School Leadership-

A Scottish Perspective

By

George Gilchrist

<u>Thanks</u>

I would like to thank all of the wonderful colleagues I have had the pleasure to work with, both within education and elsewhere. You have all helped shape me into the school leader I am today. You cannot, and should not, lead in isolation, and I am well aware that it is the daily contact and interaction that I have had with colleagues that has given me the inspiration and confidence to write this book, as well as much of the content. Perhaps it is only teachers, and those who have worked in school, who fully understand the difficulties and complexities of the work that we do. Sometimes people looking in from outside seem to think 'That's easy, I could do that' Well, in my experience people who make difficult jobs look 'easy' are the most skilled and experienced of practitioners. Thank you to you all.

Thanks also to all the colleague headteachers, and those from my local authority, Scottish Borders, who were so patient and supportive of me on my own leadership journey.

Particular thanks to the pupils and staff of Parkside, Ancrum and Newcastleton Primary schools. You helped me put all this in to practice, and ensured the journey was fun!

Lastly, thanks to Susan and all my family for the support and encouragement they have given me to actually sit down and do this, after hearing me talking about it for so long.

George Gilchrist November 2012

Contents

Introduction

"I can't imagine anything more worthwhile than doing what I love most. And they pay me for it."
Edgar Winter

My name is George Gilchrist and I am currently headteacher of two primary schools in southern Scotland. I was born to teach. I love teaching and love being a headteacher. As Ken Robinson might note, I have found my passion and I am in my element. That is not to say that the discovery of these things was easy and straightforward, they weren't.

Before I ask you to consider my thoughts on leadership, schools and education, I think it only fair that you have some understanding of how I got to the point of feeling it was worth putting these down on paper and sharing with others, and my journey to get here.

I first trained for a career in education in the early 1970s. I trained at Didsbury College of Education, which was a part of Manchester University. I remember being a part of the first Bed degree cohort, where previously, and still alongside us, prospective teachers had completed the Teacher's Certificate course, before being allowed into schools. The BEd course was four years in duration and the T Cert was available over three years of study.

I completed my training in 1975 and thought I was ready to teach. I wasn't! I had studied education alongside my major curricular area of Geography and my subsidiary of PE. I had learnt about Piaget, Dewey, Skinner, their theories and their work, as well as developing my knowledge of physical geography, social geography, climatology and how to teach and coach various major and minor sports. This was an eclectic mix of theoretical and practical studies, all of which I hoped would give me an array of skills that should equip me to teach and contribute to any primary school and local authority across the country. Certainly Northumberland were very keen to have me return and teach there. They had after all funded my four years of study in South Manchester. However, I had flown the nest and didn't, at that time, really wish to return on a permanent basis to such northerly climes!

I offered myself for employment to authorities in the North West of England, but found it very difficult to get into their Teaching Pools, as they were then known. It was from these 'pools' that schools would fill their vacancies for the next school year. All these authorities seemed very keen to fill them with new teachers that they had funded through training, just like Northumberland. To cut a long story short, I therefore found myself teaching English Language (Remedial) and Religious Education in a boy's comprehensive school in southern Manchester. Not quite what I had in mind for my career, but a first step I thought, after all teaching is teaching.

Alarm bells started ringing when I was taken to my first class on my first morning. "What do you want me to teach?" I innocently asked of the head of department who was taking me along the corridor to meet my new class. "Teach?" he replied, "Son you will be doing well if you keep all this lot in the classroom," was his rather surprising response. I was then ushered into a class of testosterone-fuelled teenagers, as he beat a hasty retreat, back to his 'A' level and well motivated students. I do remember that in that first lesson only one pupil managed to climb out of a classroom window, and he quickly returned. The rest of it I think I have erased from my memory, but it certainly felt like a baptism of fire into my chosen profession. When I arrived in the staff room at break time, there were lots of knowing smiles and polite enquiries, as everyone was desperate to hear how I got on with 3S, and how many had escaped? I'm not sure if they had run a sweep on the outcome, but a few were suitably impressed when I said only one pupil had left the room without authorisation.

I, on the other hand, was in a state of shock!

What followed was half a year developing my skills of crowd control and wondering if I was really cut out for teaching. I was asked to apply for the post permanently at the end of my stint, but I knew this was not what I really wanted to do, and was certainly not the picture I had for myself of someone who was going to make a difference in so many lives. I had established relationships with lots of the pupils, and some of the staff, but I was still dissatisfied with my lot.

I had left the safety net of home, and halls of residence, and was now in private accommodation. I was in love and soon to be married, to another teacher, and we needed a second income. I couldn't wait around for my perfect job to come to me and so when I was offered a job in selling I thought "Why not? It's a salary and I can always get back to teaching when the right opportunity arises."

That was 1976. Little did I realise that it would not be until 1992 that I would return to the career path that I had always wanted to follow. By then I had experience of working in lots of different companies, either in sales, sales management or other managerial roles. I even had a spell of some five years of self-employment and running my own company.

In truth, none of these gave me the satisfaction I was looking for, so when the opportunity came to return to teaching I jumped at it. What I would say about all these jobs outside of teaching is that they gave me a more rounded experience of the world of work than many teachers have. They also gave me lots of opportunities to see different managerial styles in operation, good and bad. I also had the opportunity to try out various styles myself and to develop ways of managing and working with people that would work for me, and eventually help me become the leader I wanted to be in schools, after I had returned to education.

By this time I was living in southern Scotland, with my second wife (not a teacher) and a growing family, two in primary school and another one on the way. The 5-14 Curriculum was just being introduced into Scotland's primary schools, and the early years of secondary. I was immediately engaged with this as a parent, and I was to become further engaged as I discovered a route back into teaching.

Apparently there was a shortage of teachers in primary schools, as Government advertisements kept informing me, so I decided it was now or never. I made enquiries and I registered with the General Teaching Council for Scotland (GTCS), as you need to do in Scotland, and contacted my local authority, Scottish Borders.

Surprisingly, there were no courses then for teachers returning to the profession after a break and I was advised to go on the Supply Teachers list and gain experience that way. The headteacher of the school my children were attending very kindly gave me copies of the latest 5-14 documents, and I read these whilst I waited for the phone to ring. This was a great help because I think I had a wider understanding of what was proposed in 5-14 compared to many teachers already in post. I had plenty of time to read the documents and develop my understanding. The teachers I met did not have the same opportunities due to the work they were already busily engaged in with their schools and classes.

Anyway, the phone did ring and I started to receive my first calls to help out schools from the Supply list, and, after teaching in a range of schools and year groups, was given a long- term Supply position. This really helped, as I was able to engage with experienced colleagues as we all struggled to come to terms with the new 5-14 curriculum. At the end of this, I secured a permanent teaching contract and my second opportunity to do the job I knew I loved had begun.

That was over 20 years ago now and for the last twelve of those I have been a headteacher, firstly at a small village school, with three classes, where I was a teaching-headteacher. I then became Head of a larger town school, with ten primary classes and four nursery classes. Currently, I remain headteacher of that school and we are now in partnership with a small village school, three classes again, that feeds into the larger one. Therefore, I am now head of two primary schools, both with their own unique aspects and separate identities, but both grappling with similar challenges, as we seek to better meet the needs of the pupils in both, day by day, week by week and year by year.

That is a brief resume of my career. You will see I have had various experiences in my working life both within education and outside. I have seen and experienced all sorts of different leadership and management styles and approaches. I have seen those that work and those that certainly don't. I have been inspired to do more and better things by people I have worked with and encountered, and I have been de-motivated, switched off and at the point of despair with others. I have learnt from them all.

What I wanted to do in this book was to share my thoughts on headship, leadership and management, particularly as it pertains to schools and education. However, the messages I am giving, and things I have discovered certainly cross over into management and leadership roles outside of education. Good management, leadership skills and practices transfer across all organisations. I have learnt much from the practices in commerce and industry, and I believe they can also learn from us, and how we manage and lead complex organisations.

What follows are my thoughts, help and advice to anyone who is interested in these important aspects of how organisations work, especially schools. All I can say is that what follows is what has worked for me and I am sure has worked for others. I am not saying copying exactly what I have done will work for you and your school or organisation, because these are all different. But I hope what follows is something to help you along in your own journey of discovery as a leader and as an individual. I hope I will give you points to consider and discuss within your own teams and structures, and perhaps a little validation for paths you are already treading.

I have included a summary of main points and principles at the end of each chapter so that you these can be used as points for discussion or further consideration.

"I challenge you to make your life a masterpiece. I challenge you to join the ranks of those people, who live what they teach, who walk their talk." Tony Robbins

Chapter1

Know What You Stand For!

"When your values are clear to you, making decisions becomes easier."
Roy E Disney

It seems obvious that as a headteacher and a leader you need to have a clear understanding of your vision, values and principles. But it is easy to lose sight of these when confronted by the day-to-day management tasks and events that flood across your desk. It is also very important that the people you work with and alongside have an understanding of what it is that drives, motivates and underpins your actions as an educational leader. You will have articulated these in a variety of ways, and to lots of different audiences, and your actions should demonstrate them on a day-to-day basis. An important aspect of leadership is your ability and willingness to lead by example. By your actions you are giving life to your vision, values and principles. Problems occur when there is a mismatch between what you say and what you do. It is no use talking the talk if you are not going to walk the walk. Then you create a major credibility gap.

All headteachers, usually at interview, will have articulated a vision for the establishment they work in, and possibly for themselves. They may also have been asked to speak about their values and principles and how these underpin their vision. Out of these emerge their aims for the school and its development and these will then be part of the whole-school vision, values and aims. These can only be decided and agreed on in partnership with all members of a school community.

We all start in post with our vision, values and principles fresh in our minds, but how often do they then become submerged or forgotten under the deluge of activities and issues we have to deal with on a daily basis? It is my contention that we cannot and should not allow this to happen. We need to create time in our very busy working lives to keep revisiting these aspects and measuring what we do against them. They should be not seen as set in stone and will need to be revisited, considered and reviewed in the light of experience, new knowledge, thinking and understanding.

I was recently on a super CPD course run by our local authority. It was called the Headteacher's Book Club and colleagues and myself came together monthly to read and reflect on various texts associated with leadership and learning. I wanted to take part to ensure I had the 'me' time I think is essential to develop my own thinking and understanding. It is always best to do this collaboratively so the book club seemed to be an obvious vehicle for this. We started out with about twelve headteachers and two facilitators and had some really interesting and insightful discussions, but over the course of the year numbers diminished. At the last meeting there were five of us left.

One of our members who came to the last meeting said she really enjoyed the course and the chance to read and reflect with colleagues. But she wouldn't be doing it again as 'its too self-indulgent. There are lots of other things I should be doing at school.' I found this quite dispiriting. Here was a committed headteacher who was feeling guilty because she was not in school dealing with day-to-day management issues. It was though she saw thinking and talking about leadership and education was a bit airy-fairy and hard to justify, to herself and perhaps others, when faced with a very busy schedule back in school. When I spoke to other headteachers who had dropped out of this course, their responses and reasons for dropping out were very similar. They had too much to do and couldn't justify a day a month, or two months, for what we were doing!

I believe we have a professional responsibility to find time for such personal development, which will help shape and develop our own thinking and therefore the development of our schools and education of our pupils.

What are the values that shape you as a headteacher and a leader? When was the last time you considered these and whether you were still being true to them? Do your actions and performance as a headteacher and leader reflect your values? Are these reflected in the school or organisation in which you work? Is there a mismatch and, if there is, what are you going to do about it? These are all big questions but ones, which I would expect us all to be asking of ourselves, and others, constantly.

If you espouse values of equality, fairness and non-discrimination, is that what your school or establishment looks and feels like? Equality of opportunity for all? Fairness for all? Equality in how all are treated and valued for their contributions? You need to keep asking your staff and pupils, is this how it feels for them? No use you just thinking this is what it is like. What's the evidence that says that is what it's really like? Your perceptions and reality for pupils and staff might be something rather different. You need to check this out and take action where necessary. It comes down to the strength of relationships and your honesty and sincerity in your actions. You should be aware that staff sometimes do not like giving honest views and opinions, if they think these may cause upset, especially with a headteacher. This is particularly true if you take on a school and staff that have previously operated with a very blatant hierarchical ethos or structure.

Make time for all staff. Tell them what they are doing well and praise them regularly for it. Take a sincere interest in each of them and help develop them as people and leaders. Don't get sucked into the deficit model often prevalent in education, where we are constantly focusing on the things we are not doing or not doing so well, instead of recognising and building on the great things we do and the things we do really well.

Our values should be reflected in how we are with children and what we are trying to achieve for them all. We wouldn't think of starting work with children by telling them all the things they can't do and don't know. Though this might have happened in the not too distant past! Instead we need focus on their abilities, aptitudes and successes in previous learning as the starting point for future learning and personal development. It's exactly the same for all our staff.

By the way, you could think of your staff as like a class of pupils. There will be a whole range of experience, strengths and abilities amongst them all. There will be things going on in their home lives, which will have an impact on their performance of their duties. They are all individuals with strengths and development needs. They will all be at different stages in their careers and their learning, as will you. All this needs to be taken into consideration when developing schools. They will all react differently and at different speeds of progress. You can only start any development and improvement from where they and the school are. Seems obvious, but this is often overlooked or ignored in the rush and push for change.

Values define you as a person and as an institution.

What of vision? You need a vision for the type of school you wish to lead and be associated with. You should have also a personal vision for you as a leader and your professional development. The two are closely connected.

You may have a clearly defined vision for yourself and a path for your career. You may be able to identify different staging posts on the route-map you have constructed for your career and professional development. Good luck to you if you are able to do this. I was never able to. That is not to say that I didn't know what I wanted to do, and what I was best equipped to do. But in my experience life doesn't always run like a smooth journey or path. There will be problems, difficulties, changes of direction, and, dare I say, crashes! All of these make us the people we are and those we become, and we have to experience them all to develop as individuals. I actually spent more than twenty years out of education, but many were in management, and when I returned to my true vocation and calling twenty years ago, I was able to bring all that experience, good and bad, and the insights from them, back with me into the schools I have worked.

What I did do was travel down different routes to get to where I am today, and all those different paths felt right for me at the time, taking everything into consideration. I still do this today and this is one of the reasons I wanted to write this book. Life is full of opportunities and experiences, not only do they shape us as individuals but they can also help us as we work with young people, in order to help them discover their own paths of development, and opportunities.

I suppose I have been a bit more opportunistic in my career progression, compared to those lucky individuals who have a plan and are able to stick to it. But I do know that I have arrived at the right place at the right time for me.

Let's get back to vision. You do need to have a vision for your school or schools. Obviously you will have a major role in helping to shape and identify this. You cannot, and should not, attempt this on your own. For it to be meaningful and shared by all, it has to be developed by all. You need to work with pupils, parents, staff, other schools and colleagues, community and other agencies to develop a vision that is commonly understood and being worked towards by all.

Some headteachers and schools do exactly this and then move on to the next job in hand from the school development plan. For that shared vision to be useful and meaningful, and to justify all the work that goes in to establishing it, we need to revisit it on a regular basis.

At my own schools we would engage with it at the start of each new session, when there were often new members of staff, and to remind us all of what we agreed we were about as a centre for learning. I would also insist that teaching staff have this at the front of their planning folders, so they were further reminded regularly of the agreed values and vision that would underpin our work. I would suggest that this vision needs to be revisited by all partners at least every three years to see if it is still fit for purpose and appropriate.

Out of your values and vision will emerge your aims for the school.

These should enable you to map out the steps everyone has agreed to take to deliver on your values and vision. They can be long-term or short-term but they should reflect the journey of personal and establishment development. They should perhaps include some statements on over-arching principles that are guiding you all as you strive to move the school forward and improve the outcomes for all your learners.

As I stated earlier, once you have identified, articulated and shared your vision, values, aims and principles these need to be used almost as an audit tool to measure practice and culture within the school. Is what we are doing matching up to what we agreed as a school community? How do we know? What has been the impact and improvement for all our pupils as a result of this? This becomes part of the school's self-evaluation process and will be reflected throughout your school improvement or development plan.

If you have developed your values, vision and aims meaningfully they then enable you to identify what changes and developments are appropriate, and which are not, for your establishment, and for you individually. I would suggest that this then puts you in a stronger position to resist those things that need to be resisted in education. It is my belief that we have not been strong enough professionally and morally to stand up for what we believe in and know to be right. Basing what you do in your schools on sound values, vision, principles and aims gives us, I believe, a stronger position to fight the fights we need to fight, and make the cases we need to make.

Being a headteacher is not an easy role to fill. We have obligations and responsibilities to so many different people. What we shouldn't lose sight of that the most important people we have those obligations and responsibilities to are our pupils. Therefore we have to be prepared to stand up for what we know to be right on their behalf. Being backed by well thought out and tested values, vision, principles and aims, aligned to our professional knowledge and expertise, best equips us to confront those who would deem to know better and might shout loudest. Everyone has a view and opinion on education, and I have no difficulties with that. But, we are the professionals and we should be prepared to justify and explain everything we do and why we need to do it.

In my experience, if you have identified your values and principles, you are focused on improving outcomes for all learners, and you can articulate and demonstrate this, at all levels within the school, people will respect and accept your willingness to defend and protect what you believe is in the best interests of those learners.

That is not to say there will not be times when you have to compromise and be realistic in your approach, but one of the many skills of a headteacher is the ability to take people along with you, feeling they have all been respected and listened to. I have had many conversations with people who have disagreed with actions I have taken, or proposed, but I like to think that I have listened to them, they have listened to me, mostly, and we reached a compromise or a way forward. But I also am aware of the things I am not prepared to compromise or move on and have said that to people when necessary. It works for me and helps me sleep at night!

Our lives can be full of difficult conversations, knowing your values, vision, principles and aims, make those easier to deal with.

"The greater danger for most of us is not that our aim is too high and we miss it, but that it is too low and we hit it!" Michelangelo

Know what You Stand For!

Main points/principles

- Your actions should reflect your values, vision and principles
- You should identify your personal values and principles
- Your school, or organisation, needs to identify values, vision and aims collectively
- These need to be revisited and redrafted over time
- Does the experience of the pupils reflect the school's values, vision and aims?
- Use your values, vision and aims to begin the self-evaluation process
- You are more able to explain and defend what

you do and why, when
these are clear
- **Be prepared to do so**

Chapter 2

Putting The Child at The Heart of All We Do

"Education is not the piling on of learning, information, data, facts, skills, or abilities – that's training or instruction – but it is rather a making visible what is hidden as a seed…" Thomas Moore

You would think that the putting the child, or children, at the heart of all we do, would be a given. After all, isn't that what schools and teachers have been concerned with since their inception? Apparently not!

We are just getting round to the realisation that what we do in schools should be shaped around the child, rather than expecting the child to fit around the structures and systems we have created. This might come as a shock to parents, and other areas of society who are not directly involved in schools or education. This might not be so shocking to those successful and contributing members of society who remember their school days with something less than fondness, myself included.

Early in my career as a headteacher, someone talked to me about their concern for my well being, should the school I was working in be visited by the HMIe (Her Majesty's Inspectors for Education) for an inspection. "Why are you worried?" I asked a little taken aback. "Well your school is so child centred," was the slightly surprising reply. "What else would you expect me to be centred on?" I enquired. He then explained that he agreed with my philosophy, but did I realise that the HMIe would expect to see lots of written evidence and paperwork to support where I was saying the school was at? He knew my priorities lay within classrooms and the practices therein, not paperwork and policies.

It had always been my assertion that the evidence to support the assessment of any school is to be found in the classrooms and through conversations with children, staff and parents. So I was not as concerned as my colleague and thought it entirely appropriate and natural that schools should be child centred organisations.

That whole episode did, however, reflect where we once were in terms of accountability only a few years ago. Thankfully, we have moved both aspects on, though it is desperate to know that it may have taken the death of more than one headteacher and the professional reputation of a number of others to achieve changes that that the HMIe have brought to their approach to school inspections in Scotland. Now practice and procedures have moved on and inspections aim to be more collaborative, supportive, and reflective, of what headteachers and schools are trying to achieve. This is great to see but I still worry about the approaches being taken south of our border in England, and fostered in other countries like in the USA.

A new curriculum and teaching focus has been introduced in Scotland through Curriculum for Excellence, and central to this is the recognition that the child should be at the centre of everything schools are about. Everything else is built up around this central tenet.

I did use to ask myself, and still do, though not as often, "If children aren't at the heart of what schools are doing, then what the heck is?" The dispiriting answer I came to was that they were very much focused on policies, structures and systems, often at the expense of meeting the needs of children which they aimed to serve. The blame for this lay not solely at the feet of schools and the leadership within them, but was a reflection of the demands made on schools by Governments, Inspectorates, Local Authorities, parents, vested interest groups and the media. All of these have for many years driven agendas in education, based on the premise that they knew best, and on the fact that we as a profession have not been strong enough to stand up for what we know to be right. All of which said to me that we had to do more to address our professional responsibilities and to take more confidence in of our professional expertise. We need to demonstrate more professional courage.

Because over so many years our focus had been deflected from the needs of the children within our schools, and meeting those needs, generations had passed through a system that provided many of them with no positive experiences in terms of developing their learning or understanding, and finding their place in the world. Young people had often gone on to succeed and achieve despite their schooling and education rather than being helped, encouraged and nurtured by the process. This needed, and continues to need, to be redressed.

Schools are very complex and dynamic organisations that need good supportive structures and systems in order to work effectively and efficiently. However, I think we have for to long concentrated on those structure and systems in a way that has been detrimental to meeting the needs of the pupils. We lost sight of what we were about, the education of all our learners to help them achieve their full potential, to develop in them a love of learning and to find their place in the world. For many years now, we have asked our learners to conform to the systems and structures we created for delivery, rather than starting from the learner and then putting in place the delivery mechanisms and structures we needed to meet all their needs. Children who fitted into the structures and model we created did well. But, for a large proportion of pupils the model chosen has became a barrier to learning, as it struggled to deal with individuality, creativity and divergent thinking. Pupils who didn't fit in frequently became disengaged, disaffected, disruptive and a problem, doomed to failure, within a system that couldn't meet their needs. We sought to find reasons why pupils were turned off by schools and education, so we focused our attention very much on these pupils, and the behaviours they exhibited. Many now realise that what we should have been more focused on was the structures and practices in schools that many pupils found, and are still finding, so disengaging.

Sir Ken Robinson, and others, has pointed out for some time now that we are employing an outdated and outmoded model for the delivery of education in our schools. They point out that what is now required is systemic and structural change to deliver the educational experience our children deserve, and need. In most education systems in the developed world, we are employing a linear model of delivery that is no longer fit for purpose. Learning and education is not a simple linear process that we can put children through, and know what we are going to get at the end. It is far more complex, diverse and messy, and our schools and practices need to change to reflect this.

The model we have employed, measures success through the use of standardised testing and counting the numbers of pupils who move on to further education and university. It is one that values some subjects and areas of study above others, when what Howard Gardener and others have shown us is that intelligence is not fixed and can be identified in various forms, all of which should be valued and are important to the development of a diverse society, which allows individuals to thrive. Going on to further education and university is a good experience and appropriate for lots of students, but not for all. We should have a model that values all forms of human endeavour and achievement and encourages our pupils to explore the full range of their abilities in order for them to better understand themselves and the world, and to find their place in it. We cannot meet the needs and aspirations of 21st century children with structures that are embedded in the 18th, 19th or even 20th centuries.

To do this we need to start from the children, where they are in their learning and understanding, and with their dreams and aspirations. For too many years and for too many children education has been a barrier to them finding themselves as individuals and achieving all that they are capable of.

A colleague of mine related an experience that she had in school that still affects her today. She is now in her early thirties. (We all have these experiences and memories by the way, good and bad.)

Whilst in primary school she decided she would like a career, which helped other people. She was naturally good with people, could empathise and liked to help. Howard Gardner would have said she was emotionally intelligent. She thought about nursing, but wasn't sure. As she got older and moved through school she learned about other health professions and liked the idea of becoming a paramedic. So she found out what was required and by the time she was well through secondary school she knew that is what she wanted to do, and what she needed to do to become one.

One day, my colleague was asked in class, by her Careers Guidance Teacher, if she knew what she wanted to do when she left school. She told him about her dream to be a paramedic and about the research she had done to find out about the work and qualifications required. His reaction was to ridicule her and her choice. "You're much too intelligent to waste your time and ability by becoming a paramedic!" he told her. He told her that an intelligent girl like her should be going on to university and thinking of a proper professional career. All this was played out in front of the rest of her class. She was embarrassed and rather crestfallen. She never mentioned her dream job again and was put off so much by the whole experience that she ended up in teaching!

No really, she is a super teacher and loves the job she does. But as she explained to me, there is still a part of her that thinks "what if?" She would be great loss to teaching and the school she is in but I know she would have made a super paramedic, and would support her if she decided to change career now and chase her dream.

I have no doubt the career guidance teacher described above was doing what he thought was best for my colleague. But, did he really know what was best for her and what would have happened if she had been encouraged to follow her dream?

If we truly focused on meeting the needs of the child and children perhaps fewer children would have experiences like my colleague. She understands now, as do we all, that life and learning is complicated and is not a simple linear process.

Yes, we are all born, age, then die, but the multitudes of experiences we have are different for us all, and shape the people we become. We have to meet challenges, we have successes, we have failures, plans work, plans don't work, we experience all sorts of emotional highs and lows and we quickly learn that life doesn't run smooth and free of difficulties and problems to solve.

Our schools need to reflect all of this and we have to provide our pupils with an experience that helps them to understand, and prepares them to be able to deal with what life throws at them. Our role in school is to help them understand the world, their place in it and to make the most of the opportunities they will have to thrive and be successful. Anything less and we are letting our children down.

Let us think about what we actually mean when we say we are putting the child at the heart of everything we do. To me this means we see the individual in every child, we see the whole child and everything around them that impact upon their learning and development.

For a number of years I have heard teachers complain that more and more they are being asked to act as social workers, or counsellors, or behaviour experts, or psychologists and so on. They complain that they are teachers and are not trained in these other jobs, and that all of this should be the responsibility of someone else. Well, experience has shown me that we must expect to fill all of these roles to some extent, at some time for a lot of our pupils.

How could we not?

To fully meet the needs of the children it is our professional responsibility to be aware of factors that may impinge on their learning and their readiness to learn. How could we really expect all children to learn and succeed in school if there are things going on in their life that are preventing them from being in the best place to learn? We need to be aware of these factors and to deal with them, as best we can, in order to meet the needs of our pupils. I am not saying we can solve, or eliminate, all these factors, but we certainly have to be aware of their impact and consequences.

I am sure we can all recall times in our own lives when personal events and circumstances were such that they prevented us from delivering the best we could in our professional lives, or elsewhere. This is what it is to be human. We have feelings and emotions and they are not always in kilter or balanced. When they are not, it has an impact. This is true for us as adults. For children the impacts can be more severe and profound, although I never cease to be amazed at the resilience of children in the most difficult and trying of situations. If children are coming to school from a chaotic home-life or emotional turmoil, they might not be in a place to learn about the differences between analogue and digital time, no matter how wonderful and multi-sensory the experience you have prepared for them! We have to accept this and see that bigger picture.

All of the above is why we need to embrace a more holistic approach to meeting the needs of the child. The needs that they might require most support with at any particular time may be emotional, social, and behavioural, or something else and we should demonstrate the willingness and flexibility to deal with these when necessary.

Yes, we will seek advice and support from other agencies and professionals to help us, but if we are the people who are with these children for five hours, or more, each school day, it will fall on to us to provide supportive interventions when and where necessary. I recognise this is not easy and presents us with many challenges, but I believe most teachers are up to the challenge and accept this as more and more a part of their role and responsibilities. It's no longer adequate to believe that what we do is all about teaching or subjects. It's about facilitating the development of the whole child, in the fullest sense.

If we do put the child at the heart of everything we do, we are better placed to be able to meet their needs and to tailor what we do to cater for these. We should know the strengths and development needs for all our pupils. Our teaching will be planned to build on previous learning and experiences in order to address development needs.

This seems another obvious statement, but one which some colleagues still find tricky. We should be focused on moving children forward in their learning and letting them see why and how this is happening. They need to recognise and understand their own role in facilitating the learning process. We should be connecting all their learning to the real world. We, and they, should recognise learning as a lifelong process and journey, not a destination. We should be focused on raising standards and attainment for all our learners. As Ken Robinson has noted, "I haven't seen a good argument yet to convince me that we should be lowering standards!"

I want all pupils to leave school literate and numerate to be able to make the most of the opportunities they wish to pursue in life. I want them to have developed and practised attitudes, aptitudes and abilities that will enable them to be successful down whichever path they travel in life. I want them to be happy, healthy and with a good understanding of themselves, with strategies for future learning understood. They should, as Curriculum for Excellence extols, be confident, responsible, effective and successful in helping to shape their world. I want them to dream and to feel confident that they have the tools and knowledge to set about achieving those dreams.

The only way to achieve this in my view is by focusing on them individually and what they need to be successful. I want them to be self-directed and independent life-long learners.

If the way we structure our learning and schools is such that it prevents most of our pupils from achieving their full potential then, to me, it is a no-brainer that we have to change what we do and how we do it. I believe we have begun this process in Scotland and other countries, as we all seek to align our education systems to the needs of our rapidly developing and changing society.

But we need to be vigilant and finish what we have started.

"All children are artists. The problem is how to remain an artist once you grow up." Pablo Picasso

Putting The Child at The Heart of All We Do

Main points/principles

- We need to ensure the child, and their needs, are at the heart of everything we do
- Pupils are more important than policies
- We need to demonstrate professional courage
- Our structures and organisation need to change to meet the needs of learners, not vice versa
- Learning is not a simple linear process
- Intelligence is not fixed
- We should value and recognise a range of different destinations for our learners

- We need to see the child holistically
- Our pupils need to be literate, numerate, and more
- We need to equip pupils to find their place and be successful in an ever changing and developing society

Chapter 3

Relationships, Relationships, Relationships!

"The secret of my success is a two word answer: Know people!"
Harry S Firestone

"Our most important resource is our staff."

How often have you heard this said at meetings, written in newsletters, stated in briefings, repeated in the media? It is true, but too often the people who say it are betrayed by their actions not their words. It is no use talking the talk, if you are not going to walk the walk!

Schools are complex organisation and communities because they are centred on people. In case you hadn't noticed, people are complex and complicated! Schools will succeed or fail to varying degrees on the strength of the people who make them real, and on the strength of relationships that create their corporate identity.

Learning is best as a social activity. Yes, there are times when we need to learn and think alone, but generally we learn best with partners or in groups. Then we are sharing the learning experience and helping to shape each other's thinking, learning and understanding.

Just as teachers and staff need to develop relationships with pupils to best facilitate their development and learning, so too have headteachers to cultivate and develop a whole raft of different relationships, and at different levels, to ensure schools are providing the best opportunities for learning and development for all pupils. Such an approach also helps staff to thrive and feel valued. It is not easy and presents us with a whole host of challenges, but, when we get it right, can also be a great source of satisfaction and pride. Conversely, when we get it wrong, it can provide us with some of our greatest challenges and cause some of our biggest frustrations.

Children and adults are all different individuals. They have had different experiences, and even when the experiences are similar they react and respond differently. This means that interactions between them all are complicated. We have learned over a period of years that we are responding, positively or negatively, to people as soon as we meet them. Body language, body shape, dress, smell, voice, attractiveness, overload our senses and brains to get us making almost instantaneous decisions about people and whether we are going to get on with them. Everyone, including us, can have lots of stuff going on in their heads, which they think and treat as gospel, when in fact, it can be absolute rubbish. This stuff is also affected by our own physical, mental and emotional state.

No wonder relationships are difficult!

When we are developing relationships over periods of time we have to be taking all of the above factors into consideration, as well as how people act and respond to us.

As a headteacher, you will have some say over the appointment of the staff you have to work with and with whom you need to form positive relationships. However, this can only happen over time as most of us inherit a staffing compliment already in place and the onus is really on us to develop the relationships with them. Not easy, as they will have already developed relationships and a collective identity.

You will have no say over the pupils and parents you have to work with. You will have no say over lots of other people at local level, and beyond, and from a host of other agencies that you also have to work with. Therefore, you will need to spend valuable time cultivating and developing all these relationships to better meet the needs of all your pupils.

So, you need to spend time on relationships. I have always been a firm believer that it is the people who make the school, not the buildings. I have seen some of the most wonderful educational experiences being provided to pupils in the most challenging of environments. Equally, I have seen some far from satisfactory ones being delivered in brand new state-of-the art buildings and settings. This is most often down to, not just the quality of teachers, but also the climate and ethos of the establishment.

For real proof that it is the people who make a school, try going in to one during the holiday period. What you have then is an empty shell of the entity it is supposed to be.

I was lucky enough to visit Malawi a few years ago. We visited various schools in the Mulanje district in Southern Malawi. Malawi is known as "The warm heart of Africa" because of the friendliness of its people and their attitude to life and visitors. We visited schools that had over 200 pupils in a class. There were pitiful few resources in these schools. Jotters were rare and shared with two or three pupils, where there were any at all. Some classrooms had old wooden desks but often the children just sat on the floor, or even outside in the school grounds. The teachers were not paid much, if they were paid at all. Whilst we were there some of the staff had not been paid for over three months!

However, the children wanted to learn, their parents wanted them to learn and the teachers wanted to teach. And they did! Children were learning in two languages, the local dialect and English. They were experiencing a mixed and varied curriculum with a focus particularly on literacy and numeracy. The main element that was making this work was the commitment, enthusiasm and skill of the teachers, who were not going to let a few difficulties, 'challenges', stop them from doing the best for the children in their charge. It is worth noting that a lot of the "challenges" they faced would have most of our staff walking out and probably not coming back!

They have a saying in Malawi and Africa that says "It takes a community to educate a child" and this was demonstrated every day. The school community and local villages where the pupils came from were determined to overcome the challenges faced by all in order to provide their children a better start in life than previous generations. Many of these children were orphans because of the widespread Aids epidemic in Malawi, but their education was seen as a community responsibility, and the best way to help give those children better chances in their lives. True evidence that, with committed people, we can achieve so much for all of our children.

In schools, headteachers need to take the time to understand and develop all the relationships needed to help shape and improve the school. You really have to start with all your staff and be seen to respect and value them all, involving them all in the development of the school, and therefore improved outcomes for the pupils.

I visit too many schools where there is an inequality amongst staff and the treatment and attitudes to them. All staff are important and valuable, because they all bring the school ethos and values to life. Equally, they have to see further development of the school and what they do, in conjunction with their colleagues, as a key element of their professional responsibilities and personal development.

Leaders need to demonstrate emotional intelligence. They need to understand themselves and the factors that affect their own performance, positively or negatively. They need balance in their own lives. Too much lip service is paid to the issue of real work-life balance. It is crucial to your own well-being and that of the school, that you have some equilibrium in your life.

If your work life becomes all consuming and is put ahead of all other areas of your life, not only do you risk becoming a rather narrow person, you are also setting yourself up for failure in these other vital aspects of your being. These include your relationships with partners, with friends and family and your health.

Being a headteacher is very demanding and it is my belief that you can only function at your best when your life outside of school and your career are balanced and relatively stable. Your career and job are important aspects of your life and your identity, but they are not the only important aspects. You neglect one area only at the expense of other areas.

On a course in Edinburgh recently I met a new, young, inexperienced but obviously able headteacher who told me she had decided a while ago that she was putting her career ahead of her social and family life. I found this very sad but perhaps a reflection of the common attitudes that have pervaded education and professional careers for some time.

Friends had told her she was wrong to be putting her priorities in this order, and that she would regret these decisions later in life. She can't see this at the moment because her overriding passion currently is her school and her career, and what she feels she needs to do to be successful.

As you can imagine, such headteachers will arrive very early to school and leave late. They can be found in school at weekends and can be relied on to take part in local authority working groups, as well as seeking further qualifications.

Not only do I believe such leaders have got their lives out of kilter, I also believe those above her, her line managers, are not giving the right kind of support and advice. Sometimes we need saving from ourselves.

I also wonder about staff in such schools, and their well being, under the leadership of such driven and narrowly focused individuals. Someone needs to think and look out for them in situations like this.

The headteacher I have described above is not uncommon. I have met many like them and they are all passionate about their jobs and their desire to make a difference in children's lives. What they don't seem to get is that they may be achieving less for their pupils because of their attitudes and practices, and the impact these have on them, their staff and the people around them.

During my own career I have had the opportunity to meet and work with lots of different headteachers and colleagues. I also had a spell of some 20 years where I was working outside of education and worked in commerce and business sectors. During all of my working life, I have seen and experienced lots of different leaders and leadership styles. Some very good and some quite appalling!

One thing I have learned, and reading has confirmed this, that organisations that are based on hierarchical power structures don't work effectively, or rather they don't work for all. It depends on where you are in the hierarchy! I have read some of Malcolm Gladwell's books over the last few years. He is fascinated by success, genius and difference. He has met and written about many people who would fit into these categories and rarely if ever have people achieved fantastic things on their own or in organisations that stifled creativity and where people were expected to know their place.

Success is achieved by building on the good work of others, working co-operatively and in situations where creativity and innovation were encouraged. You also have to work very hard and have a modicum of luck at times!

Organisations that are successful and thrive keep reinventing themselves, encourage innovation and the development of new understandings. If you try to mark time, you're going backwards! Schools are no different.

Ken Robinson and others continue to argue for systemic change in our education systems. They are right. I can't think of any successful business or organisation operating today that is still using structures that are embedded in the 19th century. But, many of our schools and education systems still do!

One of the big changes that need to happen is that our schools have to embrace a more open culture of internal and external sharing of expertise and experiences between colleagues at all levels. I saw this described as the 'reciprocity of learning' recently, and think this describes it really well. It is no longer all about the headteacher and the senior management team deciding and passing down the chain of command various edicts designed to bring about improvements in performance. Meaningful change comes from a collective recognition and collaboration with others.

Schools and education are notorious for working to a deficit model of performance. "Right, what's not working as we think it should be, and let's set about putting it right?" I believe it would be more appropriate to share and start with what is working and successful, learn from this, and use this as a vehicle to bring about improvements elsewhere. We need to get better at learning from each other and sharing our findings.

Our staffs in schools are overwhelmingly working well, so let's start from them. Every school needs to develop a culture of mutual trust and respect, where all are valued and included in evaluations and decisions about how to improve. Where good ideas, and sound research are the currency of school improvement. Where no one person is seen to have a monopoly on these and where everyone is concerned for the health and well-being of not only themselves but everyone else as well. Where mistakes are seen as acceptable and expected because how else will we ever improve and move forward? And where innovation is not only encouraged, it is expected!

We have to see the importance and currency of relationships within our organisations. Senior leaders need to see these as crucial 'glue' in the development of the school and the individuals within it. No one person has all the answers or a 'magic bullet' for school development and improvement. But, we are more likely to reach the right answers, ask the right questions and take the right path, collectively and collegiately.

The role and the impact of the headteacher are definitely changing, and need to continue to do so. Our role is now more as a facilitator for the development and discussion of school practice. Our staff are well educated and committed to their profession. We need to recognise and to tap into all the collective knowledge and understanding to help improve what we do together. We need to get know our staff well and, just as with the children, we need to look at them and their performance and development holistically. Everything that is going on in their lives outside of school has an impact on their performance in school. We need to acknowledge that and be aware, so that we can best support them and allow them to bring their best to the classroom and throughout the school.

But remember you really need to walk the walk and to be genuine and sincere in all these relationships. People can detect tokenism and insincerity and nothing will undermine morale and performance more, or destroy relationships that you have spent time developing. Spend genuine time listening to their ideas and concerns and they are more likely to be willing to listen to yours!

"Giving feedback is a highly developed skill: it doesn't take place within a vacuum but within a relationship" Brandes and Ginnis

Relationships, Relationships, Relationships!

Main points/principles

- **Our staff really are our most important resource**
- **Schools and organisations are complex because they are centred on people**
- **Learning is best as a social activity**
- **Relationships are key to the performance of a school or organisation**
- **Leaders need to spend time developing and understanding relationships**

- Work-life balance is important for leaders and all staff
- Hierarchical power structures are inefficient and wasteful of staff talent
- We need to share more, internally and externally
- We need to encourage and develop all staff as leaders
- Development should build on the good practices already in place, and use these to improve other areas

Chapter 4

Learning and Teaching

"Much education today is monumentally ineffective. All too often we are giving young people cut flowers when we should be teaching them to grow their own plants." John W Gardner

If we are really putting children at the heart of everything we do, then it follows that we need to have as one of our main focuses the learning and teaching experiences they are exposed to in our schools. Do these ensure the best opportunities for personal learning and development for all learners?

Learning and teaching should be a major, if not **the** most important, focus for teachers and headteachers in schools. I have never been a great believer in writing policies in the schools I have led. In my current two schools we have written only two in the three and a half years I have led them. One was on Homework and this was very closely linked to the other, our Learning and Teaching policy.

I can remember not that long ago where the focus in schools and for headteachers was very much on writing and having policies to cover every conceivable aspect of operating a school. When schools were inspected or reviewed this often started with an examination of all the policies that had been produced. I have sitting in my office old policies on Foot and Mouth, Bomb Alerts, use of ICT and Business Continuity! There is also one for every curricular area.

The demand requiring us to produce these was often reactionary to events that had happened in one or two schools or areas, and were more about protecting our backs than looking forwards. Thankfully this has changed over recent years and everybody's focus is more on children and what is actually being delivered in classrooms and beyond. However, I would argue that learning and teaching is one area where we do need to sit down as a staff and flesh out what the experience of learning is going to look like for pupils in our classes and schools. Effective and progressive learning and teaching practices and experiences are crucial to meeting the needs of all our pupils, and we all need to understand and have ownership of our vision for this.

Key to getting the learning and teaching experiences for the pupils to a high level is the acceptance that our aim is for the best for all

our pupils, no matter the barriers and difficulties they may face. Not just for some of them, or for most of them, but for **all** of them! This means that schools and individual teachers, and other staff, have to recognise each child as an individual, with their own strengths and development needs. Our role is to build on those strengths and address those needs. We will deal with the child in a holistic way and work with them, their parents and any other partner agencies necessary to deliver an educational experience tailored to meet their needs.

This is not an easy task, but we have to set our sights high and keep moving forward on this vision.

Unfortunately, we are still stuck with an organisational and structural framework that militates against all that we would like to achieve. We have a structure that is still seated in the past, based on a factory model and with educational development seen as a linear process. As Ken Robinson and others have pointed out, and as we all know, learning does not happen in a simple linear fashion. It is more complex than that. Children, and adults, develop and learn at different rates, and just because they were born in the same year doesn't go to mean they will be all at the same stage of development at any one time.

But, we have the structure and organisation we have, and until that changes we have to work within this to achieve the best we can for all our learners. This means we accept the wide range of abilities and characteristics of the pupils with whom we work. We recognise the different families and backgrounds, which impact on their learning and we offer teaching and learning that takes all this into account, and which provides different and varied learning and teaching experiences.

Wow! Just writing that down reminds me and hopefully you what an onerous task and responsibility is placed on the heads of teachers, headteachers and schools by society. But, just because the task is huge, complex and difficult doesn't mean we can't do it. Effective learning and teaching should ensure we are meeting the needs of all our learners.

One of the most pleasing developments that have occurred recently in schools I have experience of is the greater willingness of all to discuss and consider pedagogy. This was previously seen as something that was perhaps talked about and read about during teacher training at university. Pedagogy was not something that was often mentioned in schools, where the common attitude was along the lines of 'That stuff might be okay in university, but we have to keep things real here in schools.' I think it is great to see this change in our professional attitudes. People are much more prepared to talk about pedagogy, as it is recognised as vital in any consideration of improving and developing learning and teaching.

It is crucial to this process that teachers, headteachers and schools are focused on the art and science of teaching, and the impact of our increased knowledge that such practices have on the learning and development of all their pupils.

In my own schools it was when staff started conducting their own practitioner enquiries into their practice in the classroom that they began to become aware of the gap between their own perceptions of what was happening, and their pupil's articulation of what was really happening! They recognised that they were having an impact on the pupil's learning, but it was often a different one to the one they thought they were having. This was a real light-bulb moment for many of them.

These practitioner enquiries were to lead to a growth in personal reflection and professional dialogue between staff, key pre-requisites for personal and school growth and development. We had to face and consider some very challenging questions about what we were doing, and why. Staff began to recognise that there were lots of things that we were doing in our schools because they had always been done. But when asked to give the educational reasons, or evidence, for why they were being done, people struggled. This raised even more questions!

The whole process was very sobering in some respects but I would contend that we had to reach that stage of understanding and self-questioning before we were ready to then move forward and bring about meaningful change.

I should of course add that we were supported through this whole process by staff from Edinburgh University, and especially Dr Gillian Robinson. We began a programme of engagement with the university as a way of improving the Continuous Professional Development (CPD) opportunities available to staff to ones which were based on their needs and those of the school, following our own self-evaluation, and which we expected to have a more meaningful impact on our practice, and therefore our pupils. Through this partnership we were able to explore and engage with the latest research related to the area of the curriculum we wished to improve (Language) and our own pedagogical practice. We also engaged with colleagues in other schools and sectors, as well as within our learning community.

All staff were involved in agreeing this method of development and the high priority we wanted to give to all our learning and teaching. This was not an initiative that was decreed on high by the headteacher and the Senior Management Team. This was a development that all staff bought into and felt ownership of. After all, we were dedicating almost our entire CPD budget to take this forward. I felt we needed that level of commitment so all staff understood thoroughly what we were doing and the reasons why it was right to do it. All were involved in drawing up the plan that would take us forward. The plan was a flexible working document that we redrafted according to progress and experiences. We recognised that sometimes you have to go back before you can go forward and it is important that plans to improve learning and teaching, or any change, accept and reflect this.

I would recommend this type of approach to all schools and talk about it further in the chapter on CPD.

Once you have a plan and a focus, what else do you need to consider to ensure the highest quality learning and teaching experiences are happening in your classrooms and schools?

There has been a lot of talk and debate around different learning styles, and these have now largely been discredited. But what we do know from all of this is that children use their senses to learn and make sense of their world. As teachers we need to take account of, and remember this in planning for the learning experiences of all our pupils. It is part of the re-framing and re-presenting of learning that has to happen when our assessment tells us the child or children haven't understood the learning we have planned. Good teachers have always known this and built this understanding into their practice.

We need to consider and ensure active engagement of our pupils in their learning and the learning process. Learning is not a passive activity. How often did we use to ask children 'Who is the main person responsible for your learning?' only to get answers like 'you are.' or, 'my parents.' Now you are much more likely to get the answer 'Me!' Pupils are more understanding and aware of the necessity and expectation for their active engagement in the learning process. No longer is learning 'delivered' by the all-knowing teacher at the front of the class. It is a process that involves engagement with knowledge and information, but crucially with others, to develop understanding, thinking and creativity and the application of all this in real world contexts.

We have to seek to build the development of new understanding about learning into the learning and teaching experiences of all pupils. This means we have to develop the language of learning and thinking with pupils so that they are able to discuss their learning, and there is a consistency in understanding. We recognise the importance of metacognition and its role in learning. Teaching the children to think about and understand their own thinking, and how to develop this.

We now understand that intelligence is not a fixed state. We have to ensure our pupils realise and understand this to make the most of their potential. We need to develop their confidence, self-esteem and resilience in order to achieve and attain. We need them to have a 'can do if ...' attitude, not an 'I can't because...' attitude. We also need to ensure this is the attitude their teachers and schools have!

We have to encourage and develop in all our learners the skills, aptitudes, attitudes and abilities that will prepare them for a lifetime of learning. This will be learning in the 21st century, therefore many of the systems and practice from the 20th century, and earlier, are no longer fit for purpose. The world, and our knowledge and understanding about learning, has moved on and will continue to do so. Therefore, our practice and systems need to move on as well, as does our focus and what we see as important to equip pupils to make the most of their lives.

Learners need to recognise that learning is mostly a social process, best shared with others to enhance the experience and improve understanding and develop their thinking. Therefore we need to create and provide opportunities for co-operation, collaboration and focused dialogue, a dialogic approach, whilst learning. This will help develop deeper learning and understanding.

We need to provide them with opportunities to develop their learning outside of the classroom and in the real world. 'In unfamiliar contexts,' as articulated under Curriculum for Excellence. They have to see, and be shown, the connections between the learning inside the classroom and school, and the world in which they live. They should see the learning in school as a rehearsal and a preparation for applying this outside to help them make sense of their world and find their place and voice in it.

This is an ever-changing world, which will require them to be able to deal with change, work collaboratively, be adaptable, be flexible, demonstrate creativity and have resilience. We need the children to develop and experience these attributes in school so that they are better equipped to apply them elsewhere.

Connecting all the learning for our pupils is essential if we are to equip them for this life as 21st Century citizens and individuals. They have to see and understand the connections between the different aspects and elements of the curriculum, their learning in school, and how this will be useful to them in the real world. It is important that teachers are continually sharing this 'Big Picture' and links with their pupils, making them visible in their lessons.

Learning should be well planned with teacher and pupils understanding the learning to take place and how this builds on, and connects, to previous learning. They will meaningfully share learning intentions and success criteria, and there will be planned assessment activities, which will involve the pupils and their peers also. Planning should be sufficiently flexible to allow for change and development as the learning progresses. The planning should reflect the pupil voice, and they should contribute to planning in order to reflect their needs and interests.

Teachers and pupils should search out opportunities to deepen and develop the planned learning outside of the classroom. I believe that for too long we have tried to cover too much ground, and too quickly, and that to really deepen learning we need to take more time and allow pupils to think and assimilate new learning. We need to slow down in many respects. We are finally moving away from trying to cram our students with too much knowledge, facts and information, and beginning to focus on those more 'soft skills' that will enable them to be successful contributors and learners in any situation. In order to do this properly we need more flexibility in timetabling and planning to allow us to extend or shorten periods of study to best meet the needs of our pupils. We should plan more baseline assessment activities at the outset of any new learning in order to have a clear focus and understanding of the teaching that needs to take place.

To achieve the best for all pupils we need to ensure there is a structure to all lessons. I once heard someone use the analogy of the 9-o-clock news as a model for the sort of structure we should be looking for in lessons. We start with the headlines, what is it we are going to learn. Then we are straight into the first few items or activities. Then we should recap and recall these as we share with each other. We should then be reminded of what is still to come, followed by more items or activities. Then we need to recall all that has been covered and share what has happened and what we have learned with each other. Were there any surprises? Where do we go next and what do we need to find out about/learn next? This is one possible structure that can be used and there are many others that are very creative and engaging for pupils. As headteachers and senior managers we need to ensure there is a proper structure to learning in the classroom and across the school, which facilitates learning, and at a pace that engages all learners.

We as leaders need to constantly be articulating and leading the development of learning and teaching in individual classes and across our schools. We will use monitoring and observation activities to help us ensure this, but perhaps the best tool we have at our disposal is to develop within our schools and staff an ethos and understanding of what excellent learning and teaching looks like, and consensus that anything below this is just not acceptable.

The raising and improving of learning and teaching should be understood to be the responsibility of all. In my own schools we included and gave all non-teaching members of staff the opportunity, which most took, of joining in with all CPD and training associated with learning and teaching.

Continuous Professional Development is crucial in developing staff and schools. It is my belief that the most valuable and useful CPD activities are those that come about as a result of personal and institutional self-evaluation. From such evaluation we should be able to identify activities that develop individuals and schools from where they are and to bring about positive impacts for pupils. The days of teachers going off and doing one-off CPD activities based on the idea that they looked interesting should be gone. What we need are collective staff and schools development opportunities and activities that we know are going to make a difference for our pupils and improve what we do.

CPD doesn't have to be expensive to have an impact. One of the most effective activities you can engage in is by providing staff with time and opportunities for professional dialogue and reflection. Build this into your CPD programme to show that you value it, and recognise that it can make such a difference to understanding and practice. This should be done over time and in a culture of professional trust, free of personal judgements and criticism. It has to be seen as a way of moving forward with thinking and practice. Trust develops over time and staff can develop together and are able to support each other towards a common end.

CPD is crucial to school and personal development, so much so that I have included a chapter on this elsewhere.

We need to work together as a staff, just as we encourage such co-operation and collaboration in our classrooms. Staffs need to recognise themselves as life-long learners and develop themselves as reflective practitioners. In addition we need to extend our thinking and our pool of expertise by working closely with colleagues outside of our own schools. We need to work across schools, sectors and agencies in order to best meet the needs of our pupils. You can think of this like a group of individual computers that work well on their own, but when they get connected to others we have a super-computer, capable of achieving so much more.

There is much to consider if we are to develop and improve learning and teaching practices and I have only touched on some that I feel are vital. It remains with individual headteachers and schools to identify what it is about learning and teaching they need to work on to have the biggest impact. From this they will be able to develop a plan of implementation. As with so much of what we do, there is no one-size-fits-all approach that is going to work across all staff and schools, and in all circumstances. We can only start from where we are, and then move forward from there. All teachers and schools will be starting from slightly, or greatly, differing points. We should be wary of trying to get everyone to start from the same point as that leads to gaps appearing in provision across different settings, and with different individuals. We need to take all partners with us on this journey of change and improvement. I don't believe there is a destination on this journey as we will always be seeking a way forward and to improve what we do. There is no standing still, only backwards or forwards. I'd choose forwards every time.

"Education is what survives when what has been learned has been forgotten." B F Skinner

Learning and Teaching

Main points/principles

- Learning and teaching needs to be at the centre of school development and improvement
- Our aim is to achieve the best for *all* pupils
- Teaching to meet the needs of all is not easy
- A focus on pedagogy is important
- Staff need time for reflection and professional dialogue
- Knowledgeable and experienced support partners can facilitate growth

- Pupils need to be active participants in their learning
- Pupils should understand how they can improve
- We need to connect and develop learning to the real world, and in unfamiliar contexts
- Learning should be planned to build on previous learning
- Lessons should have a structure
- Improvement of learning and teaching is the responsibility of all
- Good quality CPD is vital
- There is no one size fits all solution, schools and staff have to start from where they are

Chapter 5

Headship, Management and Leadership

"It is impossible to give what you don't have. Invest in your leadership. Keep learning." Shawn Upchurch

I thought this would be one of the easiest chapters to write in this book. It has turned out to be one of the hardest.

Headteachers need to be able to deal with each of the above aspects separately and to see that their performance in each will identify them as a professional, and shape the school in which they operate. The reason this chapter has been so hard to write is because to get all of these elements right is a very demanding task, and might even be impossible. We all have our strengths and development needs. Things we are good at and things we are not so strong in. We all have likes and preferences, and dislikes and things we might prefer not to deal with. As a headteacher, you often have no choice but to deal with every issue that is put in front of you. Some of these you have to deal with personally and some you may be able to delegate to others, if circumstances permit. But everything is ultimately your call.

Headteachers are no different to any other individual on the planet. They have personal lives and professional lives and both of these are closely intertwined, often flowing in to each other. It is also certain that each aspect of their lives impact on each other. Just as with all staff, heads need to achieve a balance between their professional and personal lives. In addition they also need to achieve a balance within all their professional responsibilities. No easy task.

Headship concerns the ability to lead a learning based organisation in order to provide the learners in your school with the best possible learning opportunities, so that they are able to develop as individuals, as life-long learners and to be successful in their lives. This is quite a task on its own.

Successful headship involves the synthesis of professional expertise, knowledge and experience that is specific to schools and learning. This is not to say that Heads are not influenced and impacted by practices developed in other types of organisations, commerce, business, media, etc, but there is a unique element to schools and education and their core activities.

Our 'customer base' is children and parents.

An effective Head needs to be able to develop an organisation that has learning at its heart. Specifically it is the learning of children and young people. Schools are charged with providing a large part of the base-work, in terms of learning, individual and social development, that will help pupils go on to lead successful lives and make the most of their abilities and potential. The Head has to synthesise the knowledge and experiences required to bring about an effective organisation for the provision and development of this learning. They need to be concerned with not only the curriculum they provide, but also the learning and teaching experiences that happen in the school, the health and wellbeing of pupils and staff, the social and emotional development of the pupils and their intellectual development.

They have to do this in a spirit of co-operation and collaboration with the pupils, parents, local authority (for most), community and partner agencies, in order to meet the needs of all their charges. They need emotional intelligence as well as professional knowledge and experience. They need to work with colleagues and people at all levels to constantly ensure the best possible experiences for their pupils.

To achieve all this, Heads need to think strategically and plan for development to happen. Plans will be based on local and national needs and agendas, but also very much on the school's own self-evaluation process. These plans need to be constantly revisited, and redrawn, and assessed, to ensure they are having positive impacts on pupils and learning. The 'So what?' question needs to be asked all the time. So what has improved and changed for our learners? Where are we going next? How do we know and how will we know when we are being successful?

These are very big questions for schools and Heads. All the time acknowledging that learning is a messy business and children and staff are all different individuals who will impact on the activities of the school, positively and negatively.

All of the above is part of the headship role of headteachers, but there is more to the complete role than just this element.

Heads are managers appointed by school boards, local authorities or governors to manage and lead the school they are in, on their behalf. This management role of the headteacher is massive and is the demanding aspect of their role that they are dealing with on a daily basis. It's the everyday management issues that take up most of a headteacher's time and the one you will hear most complain about. "I don't know what happened to day! I had all these things planned, and I never dealt with any of them," is a familiar lament. The thing is schools are busy places filled with young pupils, parents and staff, and there are a myriad of things that can, and do, happen that need to be prioritised and dealt with immediately.

I had a day recently where I was dealing with staffing issues, behaviour problems, other agencies and parents, none of which were planned, but all of which needed immediate attention by me. When these days happen the Head just needs to accept that this is part of their role and responsibility, and to recognise that such prioritising is a key skill of an effective manager. The people who make up the community of the school should always have precedence over other areas, and certainly over paperwork and administrative tasks.

When you are not being swamped on days like the one I have described above, there are still lots of other management duties for the Head to fulfil. Nowadays, we have more and more direct responsibility for staffing and budgetary control. If we are fortunate we have experienced office and administrative staff, or Bursars, available to support us with these aspects. But we have to understand accounting systems, budgetary control and monitoring, health and safety legislation, risk assessment, human resources policies and legislation, and so on. The list can seem quite endless at times.

The latest one we have become more familiar with over recent times is Business Continuity planning. Here we prepare plans so that the school can continue operating, with the least disruption, if some catastrophe happens and we have to relocate quickly! There does seem no end to the ingenuity of companies and consultants to identify gaps in what we do already, and then to convince us, or our line management, that we need to do something about these.

As local authorities face ever more demands for cutbacks in resources and staffing reductions, so less and less support is available to deal with issues like this from the centre. This means more and more is being demanded of Heads and schools.

Management of staff is extremely important to the success or otherwise of any school. This is so important I have dedicated a whole chapter to this elsewhere in the book on the importance of relationships to school wellbeing. But we also have statutory and regulatory responsibilities and duties to fulfil with regard to our staff. Our role to oversee the quality of learning and teaching in our schools means we need to monitor and manage this. We need to support staff but we also need to deal with underperformance, an aspect that has traditionally been difficult for schools to deal with. I actually feel we are better at this now, and we have been helped in Scotland with our Standard for Registration, as provided by the General Teaching Council for

Scotland. This gives teachers and their managers a descriptor of, and measure for, teacher competence. This can be a useful tool to identify problem areas and to target support that may be required to help staff move on in their practice.

I have always believed that no-one comes to work aiming to do a bad job. Just about every teacher I have ever met has the best interests of their children at the heart of everything they do and are trying to do their best in a very demanding job. If that is the case, the very least we can do as managers is to offer them support to help them achieve this. Mind you, I do feel we should give short shrift to those who have found themselves in the profession and who hate their jobs or don't like children. They do exist, because I have met them! To be fair to them and to the children they work with, we need to get them to understand that their lives, and the lives of the children they come into contact with, are too short to waste by doing something that makes them unhappy. Children do not deserve or need to be taught by someone who doesn't want to be there and has little respect for their needs. There will be a better job or profession for these people, but they might need support to recognise this.

We have to manage other physical resources and the school estate as best we can, on behalf of our employers and the children with whom we work. It is sometimes amazing the time that can be spent dealing with smelly toilets, leaking roofs, poor temperatures and all the other problems and issues that your janitor or clerk of works will drop at your door.

Then when you do get money and resources to carry out refurbishments to aspects of the school estate, you can find yourself in the new role of project manager, overseeing the work and dealing with all the different companies and tradesmen who find it difficult to understand why they just can't come straight in and start dismantling or rebuilding half the school!

We must also fulfil our managerial responsibilities to our parents. Meeting representatives of the Parent Council, or school Boards, considering how to improve the partnership working, involving them in decisions about changing practice and moving the school forwards, considering how you report to them individually on their child's or children's progress and dealing with all the issues, that you didn't even know were issues, that they bring to your door.

All of this takes time, but is vitally important to the successful operation and development of the school, and therefore the learners within it.

Headteacher office shelves are often groaning under the weight of the files and publications that are produced at local, regional and national level that ensure they are fully up to date and informed about all the management issues they need to be aware of and deal with. Indeed, there may even be a Headteacher's Handbook produced by the Authority, but which is impossible to keep up to date, as the list of management tasks grows day-by-day and week-by-week.

So there's Headship and Management, two of the three

important and difficult roles that the headteacher must seek to fill. However, important and interlinked as these are, I believe that the third role, that of leadership, is one that we need to think about and create more time for in our already very busy working lives.

There is much written on leadership, just try Googling it or visiting your local book store to see the mountains of books written on the subject! There are lots of different leadership styles, theories and tools available to us and it is up to ourselves to find a way that works and enables Heads to provide leadership to the pupils, staff and partners in their schools

Chris Barez Brown identifies three simple ways we can lead others. We can lead from the front, lead from the middle or lead from behind. Actually, what he says is that of these three leadership positions or stances the one we use will vary depending on circumstances and with what we are trying to achieve. Whatever our predominant leadership style, we cannot adopt one that is rigid and inflexible. More, we need something that is adaptable and is changeable according to need, and which develops and evolves over time.

What I do know is that we have to demonstrate leadership. We should do this in our daily actions and interactions. We also show that we value leadership at all levels by developing meaningful distributive leadership practices throughout our schools and at all levels. We should truly recognise all staff as potential leaders and give them the encouragement and opportunities to develop as individuals and as leaders. Teachers are not just leaders of learning in their respective classrooms they can also be school leaders and should be encouraged to see themselves in that role. Support staff should also be encouraged and developed as leaders and contributors to school evaluation and development.

Leadership does require us to be aware of the differing roles we are engaged with and give sufficient time and importance to each of these. As a headteacher we have additional corporate leadership roles within the education department in which we work, and for the local authority, or our employers. I passionately believe that we have a responsibility to demonstrate leadership within the profession and to help lead and inform strategic pathways. To do this we have to engage with colleagues at local, national and if possible international, levels to explore and develop education practice and thinking. Again this is a huge ask, but I think we have to be engaged at this thinking and strategic level or we are doing the profession, ourselves, and therefore the children, a disservice. If the profession doesn't take the time to define and develop the work in which we are engaged, then there are plenty of others willing to do it for us. We might not like the results we get because of our lack of engagement!

How do we find time to carry out the demands of this aspect of the headteacher role?

Firstly, we have to see this as valuable and necessary. If we do this we will then be more ready and able to set aside time for leadership development. None of us should think that as we have reached headteacher level we have nothing left to learn, and have no more development to do. Therefore, we need to find and take part in high quality leadership development CPD activities. These may be found locally if you are lucky, or you may have to travel further afield. We, like all our staff and pupils, should be seeing ourselves as lifelong learners. I have always said the day when I do not learn or discover something new will be the day I decide it is time for me to move on and seek new learning opportunities elsewhere. I am still learning, and prepared to develop my thinking and practice.

We should look for conferences where forward-thinking or leading thinkers on education are attending and speaking. This will help develop our own thinking and understanding and to engage with, consider and question new thinking from others. We should take opportunities to be part of local, national and, if possible, international working groups and parties to further inform us, and contribute to the development of thinking and practice in education. We should be active participants in the process and delivery of professional development, not just receivers of it.

Headteachers should read! Seems obvious, but I still meet lots of colleagues who say they have no time for this. You have, you just need to manage your time better and see it as an important part of your personal and professional development, and leadership duties. Read what people are saying about education, in newspapers, magazines, including professional publications. Read books by world leaders and thinkers.

Develop your own Personal Learning Network (PLN) by getting on line. It takes very little time to get on something like Twitter and discover a whole new world of professional discussion and dialogue as I have done recently! I now am able to regularly interact with teachers, schools and educationalists, not just in Scotland, but globally. Major figures in education use Twitter and it only takes a few minutes to access them and what they are thinking. You also get access to lots of resources and articles that can help in your schools and inform your thinking. It is the 21st Century and we need to be up to speed, otherwise we'll get left behind.

Being a headteacher, and a teacher, is a very demanding but rewarding position. I still love my job and it is because of the challenges, intellectual and structural, that it poses each day that I remain committed and enthusiastic. Combine that with the opportunity to work with fabulous people, children and staff, to help them develop and grow, as individuals, and I know I have the best job in the world for me. If I also get to help shape education in any small way I can to make it more fit for purpose and able to meet the needs of our young people, and the challenges they face, then that is a further bonus, but also a responsibility.

"You are what you do, not what you say you'll do." Carl Jung

Headship, Leadership and Management

Main points/principles

- There are three main roles for school leaders
- Getting them all right all of the time is difficult and possibly impossible
- Balance in these roles, and with our personal lives is crucial
- Headship involves the synthesis of professional training, expertise, knowledge and experience in order to lead a school
- Headteachers need emotional intelligence
- Management duties can swamp our time, if allowed to do so
- People should take precedence over

paperwork and
administration
- We need to take time to
  think about and develop
  our leadership role and
  understanding
- Leadership needs to be
  flexible
- We need to develop
  leadership in others
- Headteachers need high
  level and high quality CPD
- Headteachers need to read
  and engage with other
  Heads and leaders

Chapter 6

The Curriculum

"To be educated, a person doesn't have to know much or be informed, but he or she does have to be exposed vulnerably to the transformative events of an engaged human life..." Thomas Moore

The school curriculum should be a broad, one and one which prepares pupils for a lifetime of learning and of dealing with change.

The world is a very different place to what it was in my own school days. In fact the world is a very different place to what it was ten, five or even one year ago. Our children are growing up in a rapidly changing world, which will continue this rapid rate of change as they move through school, further education and into the life of work. They will need to have the knowledge and skills required to deal with such a rapidly changing world, the problems they will face, and in order to find their place and to be successful.

We wish them to contribute to society and to develop their interests and talents. We wish them to have high attainment and to be literate and numerate. They need to be creative, divergent thinkers who are good at identifying problems and in helping to solve them. They need to be able to understand themselves and how they think. They need to recognise that they can improve their thinking, and have strategies to allow them to do this. They should be able to work collaboratively or on their own. They should be able to make connections with what they are doing in school and the real world.

They will need resilience and emotional intelligence. They will need to demonstrate empathy and understanding and to see the 'Big Picture' in everything. They will know their individual strengths and the areas they need to develop further. They will see the main person responsible for their learning as themselves and they will appreciate how to use the technological tools currently available to help their learning.

Their learning will be deep, and focused on developing in them the skills, attributes and attitudes necessary be successful in unfamiliar contexts and different situations. They will see the value of working hard to achieve in all areas. They will also recognise that there are different types of intelligence, all of which have value. They will see that intelligence is not fixed and their success will only be limited by their own expectations and efforts. They will know how to plan and set goals for achievement and to take steps towards desired destinations and achieving their goals.

The vehicle for delivering all of this is the curriculum in school and experiences and learning that pupils have when they are not in school.

Every country in the world has been looking at the curriculum that is offered in their schools to see if it is still fit for purpose. The conclusion that most are coming to is that their curriculum needs to change. Consensus in thinking is now that the old model of delivery in schools is outdated, based on an industrial design, which saw education and learning as a linear process. We all now recognise that learning is not a simple linear process. In fact learning is very messy! So we need to make structural changes in our schools, but also the curriculum needs to change to meet the pupil's needs and to develop the skills and attributes detailed above.

We need to see the curriculum as involving all the experiences pupils have, both in school and out, that develop their learning and understanding. Literacy and numeracy are still key requisites but we have more understanding and recognition now that all areas of learning should be valued, and that we shouldn't be seen to be putting greater value on some aspects at the expense of others. They are all valuable. We are taking a much more holistic view of what a school curriculum should look like, and what it needs to consider. We, in schools, need to take notice of all the self-directed learning that many of our pupils are engaged in through the rapid development of on-line technology.

I have always believed, and advised children, to find the activity or activities they love and enjoy doing, and to use these as means of enhancing their learning elsewhere, and helping them in deciding on a career path they may wish to pursue. Recent difficulties in support funding for further education mean that the traditional route into and through university is not seen as such a natural pathway of progression for all learners. Indeed many employers and companies are now running graduate level training schemes and programmes and prefer to develop staff themselves to meet the needs of the company.

In Scotland we have introduced Curriculum for Excellence as a major shift in focus for our schools and for our young learners. This is an attempt to try and meet some of the needs identified above.

Curriculum for Excellence is not the finished article. Indeed such a thing might not even exist as we are never going to cease our endeavours to improve what we do in schools and better provide for our learners. I am a firm believer that such improvement comes out of a journey of self-reflection and evaluation, and is not a destination. There will be staging posts on this journey and Curriculum for Excellence is one of these, just as 5 to 14 was another before it.

Curriculum for Excellence is radical in a number of ways. For a start, it recognises, and puts, the pupils at the centre of everything we do. You would think this would be a given in educational settings, but this has not always been the case and it was felt it needed to be stated and reflected in our new curriculum. Next, the proponents of the new curriculum wanted it to be driven, informed and shaped by the main deliverers, i.e. the teachers and schools. For too many years it was recognised that we had a top down model of delivery and development for schools and education in Scotland. New strategies and directions would be identified at national level and then these were passed down through Directorates and local structures to eventually fall to schools. They would then be charged with delivering on these edicts!

One of the key principles of the new model would be that teachers and educationalists would be given the professional responsibility to develop the curriculum which best met the needs of the pupils with whom they were engaged, using seven key principles of curricular design.

This has caused a lot of challenges and difficulties for the profession as a whole. Some have said there is not enough detail in our new curriculum and that this should have been given to us. I believe that what we have is an opportunity to really shape something meaningful at the chalk-face of learning, and to design solutions that are appropriate to local and individual circumstances. After all, all schools, teachers and pupils start from different positions, but they are all on the same journey of self-improvement and discovery. I believe it right that national government and bodies are involved in developing strategies and policies on the direction of travel in our education systems, but it is then down to the professional expertise and responsibility of us within schools and education to help shape how this can be best delivered.

In Curriculum for Excellence we have also tried to start to move away from the focus on too much standardised testing, and the attributing of grades and levels, in form of fairly meaningless letters or numbers. Instead our focus is to be on progress in learning and on the identifying of the development needs of our learners. What we have been encouraged to do is use assessment formatively to develop learning and also in a way that still allows us to report knowledgably to parents and others on children's progress. Reporting is much more seen as a whole process and not a document, and it is about giving parents and pupil's quality information about the learning that has taken place and the next steps in learning. This is delivered in the form of an on-going and rigorous narrative on a pupil's progress.

Another big change is the recognition that learning does not only happen in school. So much of children's learning happens away from school, at home, in the community and on-line. We need to recognise this and build this into our own planning and consideration. We now recognise children's entitlement to a broad general and balanced education. We should not be narrowly focused on a few academic subjects. Literacy and numeracy are still key elements of learning, but other disciplines have value also and we need to provide opportunities for these to be developed. No longer should we be focused narrowly on attainment, though that remains very important, and always will be, but we should also recognise and celebrate wider achievements. We should equally be considering the health and wellbeing of our children and how we protect this. Messages and changes that need to be embedded in everything we do and not just be seen as more add-ons.

Metacogniton features prominently in our new curriculum. Getting children to think about their thinking and how they can improve and develop this further. For all pupils to recognise that intelligence is not fixed and can be developed and that making mistakes is part of how we learn. These are aspects of the more 'soft' skills and attributes we are aiming to develop. We also recognise that these are skills which need to have transferability built into them. We now recognise the skills, attributes and attitudes we need to develop in learners for them to be successful wherever they are. These are now given prominence throughout the whole Curriculum for Excellence principles and documentation.

Subject areas are still recognised as important and valid, but so are the connections between them and the transfer of skills across them. We need to plan and teach to allow for this to happen. We need to share the 'big picture' more with children and for them to see connections between the different areas of their learning, and the wider world.

Another key aspect is the active involvement of pupils in their learning. Learning is not seen as a passive activity that is done to you. More it is seen as a process over which the individual has control and active involvement and input in to. This is recognised as being vital for deeper learning and deeper understanding to occur. When we talk about active learning, we mean this in its fullest sense. This is not just getting up and moving about, it involves being fully active in the learning process. Pupil voice is inputted into all stages of the learning process starting right from the planning phase. This has to be done in a meaningful way and not in a tokenistic way for it to be an effective part of the process. Pupils are expected to see themselves as the main person responsible for their learning.

These are significant changes in the approach being taken towards education in Scotland. However, to be truly revolutionary we would need to redesign and rebuild our schools to support the delivery of such a model. In the current, financial climate this is not going to happen. But we can take the opportunity, when new schools are being built, to explore new design concepts that will help facilitate the curriculum we wish to deliver, and this is beginning to happen, not only in Scotland but in some Scandinavian countries like Finland and Sweden.

As I said earlier, this is all a stage on a journey of continuous improvement and Curriculum for Excellence is helping to move forward our thinking and our practice in Scotland, as are similar vehicles in other countries.

"One of the greatest problems of our time is that many are schooled but few are educated." Thomas Moore

The Curriculum

Main points/principles

- The curriculum in school needs to be broad, combining knowledge, skills, understanding and experiences
- The curriculum will be holistic and include all a child's learning experiences
- It will seek to deepen learning and understanding
- It will recognise that intelligence is not fixed or one dimensional
- It needs to develop and evolve to match the changing world
- Schools and teachers need to engage with and shape curricular change
- It should provide more focus on developing

learning, identifying next
steps and the development
needs of all pupils
- **It should encourage active
participation by all
learners**

Chapter 7

Working With Parents

"Sometimes it is not enough to do our best, we must do what is required."
Winston Churchill

Where do we start with parents? When I am talking about parents I am also including guardians, carers and others who have responsibility for the children we teach.

Firstly, we have to acknowledge that without them we would have no children in our schools and, just as importantly without their co-operation and support we will not be able to achieve all that we can for their children.

There was a time, and should still be in some eyes, when parents were seen as unwelcome intruders within the gates of our schools. They were to be just about tolerated as a necessary by product of schooling children. They were to be in no doubt of their place, which was at the school gate and with a clear understanding that teacher knows best.

To be honest, most parents bought into this ethos, where they knew their place and accepted that it was the school and teacher's jobs to get on with educating their children. I can remember in my own school days where you dare not tell your parents you had been in trouble in school and be expecting any support from them on your behalf. As far as they were concerned the school and teachers knew best and if I had been in trouble I must have been up to no good, and I would face further punishments from them, just to make sure I got the message! Possibly one of the

reasons I have less than fond
memories of my own school days.

Thankfully, times, understanding
and practice have generally moved
on since my school days and we
now recognise the key importance
of the partnership between teachers,
schools, parents and pupils if we
are to try and realise each child's
learning potential. Teachers and
schools want to actively engage
with parents, as we understand how
this engagement enhances the
prospects of the children
succeeding with their learning and
development in all areas, both in
school and outside.

We now communicate regularly
and in a range of ways with
parents, and this is very much an
on-going process. No longer are
they waiting for the end of year
report on their child's progress, and
the annual parent's evening to

discover how their child has been doing in school. Now we communicate from day one of their arrival in school, and indeed we begin the process even before the children are in school, so that the parents have a constantly updating picture of how their children are doing. They should know what the children are doing, why they are doing it, what they will be doing next, and how they the parents can support them through all of this.

Before children enter primary school and nursery, or reception, classes, we will have met with parents individually and in groups beginning the process of engagement regarding their child's education and development. We will be getting to know them and wanting them to get to know us, and to see how much we value their input and the partnership working. We will be giving that important message about how crucial it is that we work together to support their child, or children. We want them to feel comfortable with the school and us. We don't want schools to be intimidating places, parents need to feel comfortable and active participants in the process of educating their children.

This is not always easy. Some will be reluctant to engage with us because of their own memories and recollections of their time in school. We are still dealing with generations of parents who do not have happy memories of their school years and we have to deal with that. I always start with new parents by telling them about how much schools and education have changed since they were in school themselves, no matter how young they are. I point out that this is the case even if they themselves went to the school their child is about to enter, and this was only a few years ago, which can often be the case.

From the outset of our initial contacts we are building relationships and developing understandings that are going to be crucial in supporting their children and themselves in order to achieve the best results for those children.

Once the children arrive in school, we will be having daily face-to-face contact between teachers, senior management and parents. We augment direct contact with parents through school newsletters, handbooks, websites, class-newsletters and other streams of information, as we seek to give the parents as much information as possible, and in different formats, about the progress their child is making. In my own schools we have 'Meet the Teacher' meetings very early in a new session, so that parents can meet their child's teacher, hear about plans for activities and work planned for the new term, look at resources that will be getting used, hear how they can support their children and ask questions or seek advice on how they can provide such support. This process of sharing information and two-way communication develops and continues over the rest of the school year, and indeed over the full time a child is in the school.

The two-way aspect is important and I am always talking to parents about how crucial it is that they speak to us early when difficulties arise. If children are having difficulties at home or school it is really important that we are aware and we share relevant information. Hopefully, difficulties in school will have been picked up by teachers and will be getting dealt with. Whenever there are such difficulties, it is always important to inform and involve parents. This may be low-key involvement by the class teacher speaking to parents to make them aware, advise what support is being given and share strategies. It can be at a higher and more formal level involving senior management, other agencies and parents but the principles remain the same. Identify the issues, decide on appropriate support required, monitor and review when necessary and reassure parents and pupils that we are all working together to help overcome possible barriers to learning.

Often though, the difficulties a lot of children face can stem from circumstances outside of school. These tend to create emotional and social obstacles that can become barriers to learning and have to be recognised and dealt with, before a child is able to achieve their potential in learning. It is crucial that there are open lines of communication between schools and parents to deal with issues effectively when they occur. That is why I am constantly advising parents to come and speak to us confidentially when things are going on in pupil's lives that may have an impact on their ability to learn. We need to know, so that we can take the necessary actions to allow for and accommodate this. If parents are going through a messy divorce, one is seriously ill, they are short of enough money for basic necessities, or some other circumstance is pertaining that can seriously throw a child's equilibrium, then it can be completely unrealistic for us to expect them to behave and concentrate normally in school. We need to make allowances and adjustments according to the circumstances or situation. To do this we need to be informed.

I would contend it is more likely that we will have the information required, if we have developed an 'open culture' with easy lines of communications. I do recognise that such an 'ideal' situation will not prevent the occasions happening where pupils are not engaging and we 'know' something must be going on elsewhere in their lives, but nobody is telling us what. This can be because of denial by parents, they don't know how to tell us, or for other reasons. Whatever, we will be dealing with the consequences in school so I think it important that we try and create a culture and systems that make it easier for parents to share information with us sooner rather than later.

Throughout the school year then, we will be sharing information with parents. This will not be just what is happening and when, but will be giving them information about the rationale behind what we are doing. It has become increasingly common for schools to have 'Curricular Evenings' for parents to share latest thinking and developments in aspects of curriculum development, teaching and learning and assessment. As we improve and develop our own understanding of what and how we do things in school, it is imperative that we keep parents up to date with the changes that are happening, and the reasons why we need to change.

In Scotland we have been introducing and implementing Curriculum for Excellence for a number of years now. One aspect I think where we have let ourselves down with this development is in keeping parents informed and on-board with the changes that are happening. Some of the changes are pretty profound, especially in the secondary sector and in the exam system. Parents have been very anxious about some of these changes, but I feel that a large driver for this anxiety was a lack of information given to parents by schools, local authorities and Scottish Government about the proposed changes. Some may argue that schools were struggling to give information on some aspects because of a lack of information they had themselves, and this is true in some areas. However, I do feel we didn't help ourselves at times by our slowness to engage with parents on the changes happening, at all levels.

So, at school level it is important that we keep parents up to date with change and developments happening. This means more than just sharing our latest School Development Plan and Quality and Standards Report on a yearly basis, but should involve regular updates and consultation on what is happening. We are much more likely now to have parents on working groups looking at particular developments, and working alongside teaching staff. This is not only helping them see the school development as a whole, but is also helping to inform them about areas the school is working on that will help impact on their own child, or children.

We are now more likely to have two or more parent's evening over the course of the schools session. In my own schools we adjusted how and when we arranged these following consultations and work with our Parent Council, and other parents. We have a Parent's

Evening in November, when we discuss how the children have settled and the progress they are making, and look at work already undertaken. We produce our main report for issue in early March. This is a report on the year to date, details progress made in learning, identifies next steps and considers the pupils attitude to, and understanding of, their learning. It will also share and recognise other achievements both in school and out.

Parents had asked us for the main report in March as they felt an end-of-year report in June left no time or opportunity to deal with any issues that had arisen. Staff and I could see the sense behind this and so we agreed to trial the suggested change, then we will consult with the parents again about how they found this? We also have an Open Evening in June, when parents and pupils come in to school to see and hear about the work produced over the school session.

In addition to the above reporting procedures, we also have our regular curricular newsletters going home from each class, once a term and these are also shared on the school website. We have Christmas concerts, individual class assemblies, Scottish Culture days, enterprise days, forest school activities and an end-of-year celebration as some of the many other ways we are involving parents in the life of the school, informing them and demonstrating the progress their children are making in their learning.

All of the above is part of the constant dialogue we are having with parents as we seek them to be more informed and more involved in the learning process for their children. I have no doubt that we will continue to develop these even further, and the use of Social Networks, websites and systems can be utilised to develop this further in the future. We have to keep reaching out and developing these relationships for the betterment of what we do and for improved outcomes for all learners.

That is not to say that developing such relationships and avenues of communications with parents is easy. Its not, and no matter how many different ways you try to facilitate that interface and connection with parents, there will still be some for whom its not enough, and you still will be unable to reach. What do you do about those parents who refuse to engage, for whatever reason? One thing I do know is that you can't give up on them and you still have to keep reaching out to them. After all, it's not about them it's about the children. If you really believe that you can only achieve the very best for pupils with the active co-operation and engagement with their parents and guardians, and I do, then you cannot give up in striving to reach out and engage with them all.

"Set your goals high and don't stop till you get there." Bo Jackson

Working With Parents

Main points/principles

- Without co-operation and partnership with parents, pupils will not achieve the full potential in their learning
- Parents are very much active partners in the learning process
- Communication links need to be regular and varied
- Relationships need to be established based on trust and understanding
- The dialogue with parents needs to be two way
- We need to be aware of things going on in a child's life that may affect their ability to focus and learn
- We need to engage with parents individually, collectively and consistently

- **We need to keep reaching out to them all**

Chapter 8

School Development and Self Evaluation

"Progress is impossible without change and those who cannot change their minds cannot change anything." George Bernard Shaw

I touched a little on school development and self-evaluation earlier but because of its crucial role in driving through change and improvement in what we do, I feel we need to consider this in a bit more detail.

As I have already stated, schools cannot stand still. If we are not moving forward in what we do, we are falling backwards and behind those who are committed to improvement. This can be other schools or other countries. We live in a smaller and smaller world because of developing technologies and our pupils are not just competing with pupils from other schools in their own countries for opportunities and employment, they also more and more have to compete with their peers from other countries as well. We need to recognise this, and the fact that other developed and developing countries are seeking to improve the education they provide their young people to increase their choices and chances of success. We have to do the same, as a country, as local authority, as individual schools and as individual teachers, otherwise we risk falling behind and failing to meet the needs of our young people. We should see the drive to do better as a process in which we are continuously engaged.

That thought can seem very overwhelming for some, and would be for all, if we were unable to see how we can possibly deliver on such an unrelenting and demanding desire to improve and get better. Fortunately, I feel we have developed and become so much better at planning for achievable school development, using improved understanding and practices in self-evaluation and development planning to help us achieve this.

I remember when we first started to look at and think about planned self-evaluation this was quite an alien process to many. We were used to outside agencies, like the HMIe or local authority, coming into schools evaluating where they thought we were at, and then giving us advice about what they thought we should do next. The 'done to us' rather than 'by us' approach.

Then, headteachers, and senior management teams, came to recognise the value of their role in evaluating where the school was and identify where it needed to go next. They got quite adept at using various tools provided to carry out self-evaluation and then draw up a school development plan based on this, and including what the LA, HMIe and Government also thought we should be doing. This was a time when we were submerged in audits and questionnaires of various kinds, and school improvement plans were quite substantial tomes that were not read by many and were not achievable by most. It was all about the paperwork, and the more you had, the more likely people were to be impressed.

However, we probably had to go through that stage to really begin to understand and think about what we were doing and for what purpose. Schools quickly became overwhelmed and dissatisfied with what they were doing. It made sense on paper. You needed to know where a school was at in order to plan a way forward to develop and improve those aspects we were dissatisfied with. Trouble was, we lost sight of the main driver, which was to improve outcomes for pupils. Once we started asking ourselves the question 'What has improved or changed for our pupils, and where's the impact for them?' was when we really began to get a proper handle on how we should go about conducting meaningful self-evaluation, and deliverable school improvement plans that had positive impacts for pupils.

We realised that for self-evaluation to be really meaningful we should be involving the whole school community and partners in the process. So it was not just headteachers and senior managers who carried this out and were involved, but it should involve everyone engaged with the school, including the pupils! We recognised we couldn't really evaluate where a school was without having the 'voice' of all partners reflected in that evaluation. All staff became involved in evaluating the performance of the school. We also involved pupils, and found ways of capturing their voice in the school's self-evaluation processes. Parents became involved and were consulted to collect their views on the school, its strengths and weaknesses. The local community was involved and we began to speak regularly to their representatives, some linked directly to the school and others not so closely connected. Partner agencies were asked for their opinions and thoughts on the school. Other schools and sectors were consulted in learning communities, and in my own local authority we took part in the LA school review process to get even more information and feedback on the school and its performance.

All this really did mean we were getting much more of a 360 degree picture of the school and from all angles. This was a big step forward, as we felt that we had a much fuller picture of our schools than before and were able to confidently identify areas of strength and areas for development. What I and others also recognised was that it was impossible to carry out such evaluation once a year, usually around May, in any meaningful and sustainable way. Self-evaluation has to be ongoing and embedded in the ethos and practice of what we do. It has to be an ongoing process that informs the work of the school. It also has to be focused on what has changed and improved for pupils, and on what needs to change to make things even better for them. And, how we will we know when we have achieved this.

Once self-evaluation becomes accepted as part of what we do, as described above, it leads to changes in practice that are focused very much on making things better for pupils. So you get teachers being more reflective in their teaching, planning and assessment, and more able to see and articulate the small changes they need to make to improve what they are doing. Support staff come to see that they too are key partners and will reflect on what they can do to help improve the school for the pupils. Pupils themselves become very thoughtful about what goes on in the classroom and the school, as they know they will be asked, and proper notice taken of their views and opinions. Parents are more engaged and more willing to support the school, and provide ideas for how we can improve. This becomes the norm for all partners.

All of the above provides a rich array of evidence of exactly where a school is at in its journey of development and enables the school to draw up a meaningful and workable school improvement plan based on this rich array of qualitative evidence.

Every journey has to start from where you are, so it is really important that you have an accurate picture of exactly where you are before you begin that next step on the journey. Good, embedded self-evaluation should give you that starting point.

From self-evaluation you are then in a place to identify the priorities for your school improvement plan, or development plan. This plan should be driven by your self-evaluation processes and procedures that have revealed what has been successful and what you need to address next. It should be realistic, achievable and measurable, and should build on the previous plan. You still hear the voices that say 'That's all well and good but we still have to include the LA priorities and the national priorities.' They point out that this means the plan stops being the school's plan but becomes something else, as well as undeliverable.

My response to this is that the local authority and national priorities are always going to be very similar, and the school plan should always fit into these. In Scotland, as I have said, we have been engaged with Curriculum for Excellence for some years now. What does this entail and how have we made it fit the local context, or vice versa?

As the name implies, one key element is curricular development and improvement. We have examined our curricular structures to see if they are fit for purpose. Something we have always done and will continue to do. So we have been able to retain a focus on literacy and numeracy, and also to consider other curricular areas and how we can link these together in meaningful cross-curricular contexts and learning experiences. Such a focus has always been a key element of school development plans, before Curriculum for Excellence, and will continue to be so after we stop talking about the curriculum in these terms.

We also need to consider how to improve learning and teaching experiences for all pupils and the pace and challenge within our lessons. When are we never going to be focused on this in some way or another? In my own schools, and our learning community we decided to use Reuven Feuerstien's Mediated Learning approaches and the teaching of Cognitive Functions as a focus for learning and teaching development across schools and sectors. We could have quite easily have used Accelerated Learning, Active Learning, Creative Learning, Bloom's Taxonomy, De Bono's Thinking Hats, Formative Assessment strategies, or some other suitable vehicle to hang our focus on. What you do realise after consideration of such approaches is that there is much overlap in all of these. The point was, we were having the improvement of learning and teaching as a continual and central focus of our school improvement planning, whether we call this Curriculum for Excellence or something else.

Curriculum for Excellence also asked us to consider assessment in all its forms to support learning, Assessment of learning and assessment for learning. How we gathered evidence and how we reported this to parents all needed to be reconsidered and developed where necessary. Again, I can't remember a time when we haven't been considering all of this and debating about how we can improve what we do. How could you possibly look at the curriculum and learning and teaching without considering assessment as part of that process as well?

How could you not consider, and change, the key elements above without also considering planning and the quality assurance of what we are doing? You can't, because all of this is not just about Curriculum for Excellence it is about meaningful school improvement and the developing of what we do to best meet the needs of our pupils in a rapidly changing world. The priorities identified, and the strategic direction given, by the local authority are going to be encapsulated in these aspects of development too.

Therefore, it is my contention that it is still possible to remain true to meaningful school self-evaluation and also deliver what is being asked for at a local authority and national level. This is as long as we are all focused on the things that really matter and how they impact on our pupils.

If your self-evaluation and improvement planning are strong, I would argue it is easier to resist the swings of political and media opinion and pressures in order to remain focused on the things that we know to be critical in school and educational development. This is something that I believe everyone in schools and education, but especially leaders, need to get better at and be more prepared to do. You never know, we might even reach the stage where we have no external validation and inspections of schools, as in Finland. After all, who should really know the schools best but ourselves?

"One way to keep momentum going is to have constantly greater goals." Michael Korda

School Development and Self Evaluation

Main points/principles

- **Schools cannot stand still**
- **Self-evaluation is key to production of meaningful school development plans**
- **Self-evaluation needs to be a constant and ongoing process**
- **It should involve all to give a 360 degree picture**
- **The main driver for school improvement needs to be improved outcomes for all pupils**
- **We have to start from where schools, and staffs, are**
- **School priorities should link easily into local, regional and national priorities**

Chapter 9

Continuous Professional Development

"Innovation distinguishes between a leader and a follower." **Steve Jobs**

Continuous Professional Development (CPD) is crucial to personal and organisational change and improvement. It should be one of the main means by which we grow and develop our knowledge, understanding and professional competencies. At its best it can also facilitate the change, growth and development of the whole school, to better meet the needs of our learners.

CPD has been provided, at school, district and learning community, local authority and national levels, for many years. Large amounts of time and resources have been put into CPD as everyone recognised its importance in continuing to develop staff once they were in post, and after completion of their initial teacher training. Teachers recognised the need to keep up-skilling and updating their initial training, and indeed recognised the gaps that there had been in such training now they were actually in post and having to deliver on a day-to-day basis.

We have seen a massive growth and development in our understanding of how the brain works, how children learn, the impact of our pedagogical practices and how these can be improved, the importance of assessment, factors that impinge on the learning environment, and lots more that impact on learning. We have coupled this with an ongoing need to review and revise our curriculum and its delivery and the ever-changing requirements of a rapidly evolving society. This has meant that everyone in education and schools recognise that it is through continuing high quality CPD that we can best equip schools and staff to meet these challenges and demands.

Unfortunately, what came out of this recognition was a plethora of CPD courses and providers, who attempted to meet the needs of schools and staff. Some of these were excellent and some less so. Some had an impact on individuals, and within their classrooms, and some might have even achieved a little more than this. But all too many had no impact either for the individuals who attended them or, more importantly, for the pupils and schools in which those individuals worked.

I myself can remember a fabulous six-week Canadian canoeing course I did on the River Tweed, provided by the local authority Outdoor Education staff. I and the other course participants had a fabulous time. The course took place as a twilight session in the summer term. However, there was a massive disconnect between what we were doing and the day job. We all completed the course successively and returned to our respective establishments and most, like me, have never been in a Canadian canoe since and never were called upon to share their new skills with any children.

This is how most CPD was, and how it was perceived. It was a personal thing and you looked for activities and courses that appealed to your particular interests, with not a lot of thought on how these might help you become a better teacher or improve outcomes for your pupils, or help develop your school. Indeed, there was no real expectation that this should be the case.

Thankfully, times and our views and thoughts on CPD have changed a lot. We still value CPD but its value is identified in how it will develop an individual and their practice, how it will help a school develop and move forward, and, most importantly, how it will lead to improved outcomes for pupils. As a headteacher, these are the criteria by which I now judge CPD activities and requests from staff.

What we have also recognised is that high quality CPD has to be connected to the Professional Review and Development (PRD) process, which is in turn a big part of the school's own self-evaluation processes. Certainly I, and many colleagues, have recognised that much of this CPD can be, and needs to be, provided and developed in-house. No longer is CPD seen as solely something we went off and did elsewhere, but we see how it can be built into our school development programme and delivered in school, or locally in collaboration with others. When this happens, and is done well, it can have massive positive impacts on individuals and across the school for all pupils.

For the last two years the two schools I work in have been engaged in a project with Dr Gillian Robinson and Edinburgh University. This project started as a result of our need to focus on improving what we were doing in aspects of Language teaching across both schools. We had identified this as a result of our own self-evaluations and wanted to prioritise and build this in to our development plan. The SMT and I met with Gillian and spoke about what we felt the issues were and how she might be able to help us to develop and move forward. Out of these discussions came a proposal that we took to the staff of both schools. This was that, in the following school year, we would focus on the teaching of aspects of and genres of reading and writing, and to consider the impact of pedagogical practices on these. The central approach was one of Practitioner Enquiry in order to improve understanding and practice. This would be supported by Gillian, and would be demanding in terms of commitment and expectations for all. This would form the main part of our development work, would use all our CPD time and all of our CPD budget, and more, to deliver. Because of this, it was put to all staff that if we were to take such an approach everyone would have to commit and be convinced that we would bring about improved outcomes for all pupils.

We had a lot of professional discussion about this proposal but immediately we could see that all staff were excited about the possibilities, and they duly agreed to go ahead with this project.

We planned out In-Service Day times and CAT (Collegiate Activity Time) sessions over the course of the year so that Gillian could come in and work with us all. A key part of the project involved a lot of professional reading and dialogue by teachers, so that they could understand and see where the rationale and evidence came from for asking them to identify changes to what some of them had been doing for many years. This was a big challenge, when we asked teachers 'What are you doing and why?' Then to ask them to consider that if they couldn't come up with sound reasons for what they are doing, based on research and evidence, perhaps they needed to stop doing those things and do something else!

What they realised pretty quickly was that there were lots of things they were doing on a day to day basis, because they were what had always been done. It was 'Aye been' as they say in Scotland. But when they looked closely at what they thought these activities were delivering for the children and their learning, they realised they often failed to deliver these outcomes. I can tell you that such a realisation can be quite devastating for a teacher to see. But you have to have that insight and understanding before you can move forward.

I do not want to go into a lot more detail about this particular project, just to say that no other CPD work or approach that I or the rest of the staff have been involved with has produced such a marked change and improvement in outcomes for our learners. We can, and have, tracked the improvement in writing across both schools. We have tracked the improvement and understanding in reading across both schools, both of which started from high levels already. And, we have monitored and tracked the development and changes in pedagogy as a result of this ongoing work. Last session all teachers took part in a focused professional enquiry into particular aspects of their teaching of Language skills, again with profound impacts. This session they will be carrying out further professional enquiries into aspects of their own maths teaching, as we seek to develop further the culture of reflection, enquiry and professional dialogue that now exists within both schools.

The big winners in all the above work are the children, the school and the individual teachers.

So this is what meaningful CPD can deliver when it is driven by the needs of the individuals and the schools in which they work, and when it is measured on its impact for the learners. Fortunately for us in Scotland, whilst we were underway with our project, The Donaldson Report on teacher training and CPD was published and it was reassuring to note that this backed up and supported our own thoughts and experiences from our work and suggested a very similar model as a good way forward for schools and personal and professional development.

That is not to say this Practitioner Enquiry model is the only model for effective CPD delivery, there are others. But, I do feel crucial to success is that all staff buy in to what you are trying to do, and time and importance is given for professional dialogue to flourish, take place and facilitate such development. As with anything, there will be setbacks, but you accept these, deal with them and move on, whilst recognising you might have to move back or slow down to move on in the future.

I also feel that there is a further responsibility on senior managers and headteachers in schools to be just as focused and considering of their own CPD and development needs. It is one of the difficulties of headteachers and senior leaders in being able to find suitable CPD activities which are going to develop their own understanding and improve performance in order to improve outcomes for pupils. But I think the process should be the same. Start from your own PRD and self-evaluation process to enable you to identify where the gaps are and what is going to be useful to you, your school and your local authority.

In my own authority we have introduced a Leadership Development Programme that stretches across all departments of the authority, not just Education. There is a lot of merit in this and it certainly can take people out of their comfort zones. I think we need to look at leadership and management in different departments and different industries and organisations so that we learn from each other. One of the difficulties with in-house programmes like ours is we found Education Department leaders were so far ahead in terms of the whole process of leadership development, we could spend most of our time supporting colleagues from other sections with limited opportunities to further our own development. This is one reason why I think we need to engage with other organisations, in both the public and private sectors to develop our own practices.

Headteachers need to consider the three main roles, headship, leadership and management, and seek opportunities to develop across all three. You can do a lot of this independently, but the best results are achieved in collaboration with colleagues. I am a member of a Headteachers Book

Club mentioned earlier, which is an excellent way to carry out new reading and research, developing your thinking, and then to explore this further through dialogue with colleagues. As leaders we have a responsibility to be looking ahead and engaging with cutting-edge thinking and research, and to contribute to this dialogue and understanding where we can.

I would qualify all of the above with the reminder that we can only do what we can do in the time available. There will be times and issues that prevent you from doing all that you want to do. You have to accept this, remember to get that work-life balance right, and get back on track when you are able to do so.

"If we did the things we are capable of, we would astound ourselves." Thomas A Edison

Continuous Professional Development

Main points/principles

- **High quality CPD is crucial to personal and organisational change**
- **Our knowledge and understanding of how the brain works and the impact of pedagogies is continually developing**
- **Curricular change needs to occur to reflect changes in society and the workplace**
- **Many one-off CPD courses are no longer fit for purpose**
- **High quality CPD should develop individuals, their practice and improve outcomes and experiences for pupils**

- CPD should be identified out of the PRD and self-evaluation process
- CPD should sit within the improvement agenda of the school development plan
- Meaningful CPD can often be delivered in-house or locally
- Sometimes we need to slow down, or even go back, before moving forwards
- As with everything, balance is important.

Chapter 10

It Worked for Me!

"Whether you think that you can, or that you can't, you are usually right." Henry Ford

In over twenty years of teaching, including over fifteen in management, and with another almost twenty years in management in the commercial sector, I have learned many things about leadership and management.

What I have tried to do in this chapter is encapsulate lessons I've learned and insights I have gained. The following are strategies that I have found to work in lots of different situations, enabling you to be the best leader or manager you can, giving you the best chance possible to get the most out of the people you manage, and which promotes development and commitment in them.

Strike Early!

As soon as you become aware of an issue or a problem, take steps to deal with it while it's minor. The worst thing you can do is to ignore such issues and hope they will go away, or that someone else will solve them. This very rarely happens. If you, as leader and manager, do not take steps to sort out minor issues, they can quickly escalate and threaten the harmonious and effective working of the whole school or organisation.

When issues and problems are small they are easy to deal with. Often they can be solved by a simple acknowledgement or conversation before they grow arms and legs. In my experience, if you

don't deal with issues early, when
they're often quickly solved, you
will then have to spend a lot more
time, and create a lot more
disturbance to what you are trying
to do, further down the line. So,
don't do it!

Tread The Boards!

To be aware of, and able to deal
with issues, means you have to
have a sensitive 'feel' for the
'mood music' and nuances within
your school or organisation. The
only way you can develop this is by
establishing relationships, and
getting out of your office or
headquarters. Make time to get
away from that desk, computer and
phone to speak to the people who
really matter to the efficient
operation and running of the school
or organisation.

When you are meeting and talking with staff and pupils, you really need to listen to what they are telling you. That means you listen to what they don't say as much as the things they do. Check out body language and displayed levels of comfort with you and others, as a measure of the atmosphere and how people are really feeling.

How are you really going to 'know' your school if you spend most of your time in your office? Get out and about and be a regular visitor to classrooms, formally and informally.

Show Your Ignorance!

I have already acknowledged that schools are complex organisations, dealing with complex issues. No one has all the answers to all the questions that will be raised. Headteachers and leaders should not be afraid to admit when they haven't got the answer to a particular problem. Often the best solutions are found through such an admission followed by the collective consideration of the Head and colleagues. If this strategy does not provide a solution, you then need to broaden this consultation outside of the school or organisation, to engage with others who may be able to help.

I have sat in hundreds of meetings, courses and conferences, where rooms full of headteachers and leaders have listened to speakers who they have not understood or not agreed with, and no-one has said anything till after the meeting, course or conference was over!

When you are new in position, you're inclined to think you are the only one who doesn't understand

what's going on, or being said.
You're not. There are lots of
reasons why headteachers and
managers will sit in such situations
and not say anything. These are
connected to insecurity, afraid of
being 'found out', not wanting to
be embarrassed, not wanting to
upset others, playing political
games, not rocking boats, and so
on. But, you have to speak up to
help, not only yourself and your
staff but also the organisation you
work for.

Put Your Hand Up!

People make mistakes. Everyone
does, its part of the learning and
development process. As a
headteacher and leader you are not
immune from this. The important
thing is to recognise this fact, own
up when it happens and learn from
the experience.

The worst thing you can do is realise you are wrong but keep ploughing on with that direction of travel, because you are afraid of losing face. You can bet that if you have realised you have made a mistake so have others. Remember to practise what you preach. If you want staff and your school to innovate and take risks, you accept they are going to make mistakes. Similarly, you should think of your own efforts in the same way.

It is good when you spot your own mistakes, but there will be times when it is someone else who sees it before you. Hopefully, you have created a culture where they will feel its fine to have a quiet word, if it's a staff member. But it can of course be a disgruntled parent, line-manager or other, and then you just have to take it on the chin and deal with the issue raised. If you can see you have made an error, admit it

apologise, learn and move on.
Don't put yourself in the position
of trying to defend the indefensible.

<u>Be Prepared To Steal!</u>

Once you have been appointed a
headteacher or manager you begin
another period of learning and
development. We really need to be
life-long learners in all respects.
One of the best ways to learn as
such a leader is to talk to, listen to,
learn and take from others. This
doesn't just mean other
headteachers, it also means anyone
who can help you develop as a
leader, manager or headteacher.
You will have learnt much already
in co-operation with others, you
need to continue and develop this
further.

This is not to say that you will try
to become a model or a clone of
some other particular leader. That

wouldn't work and would be detected as artificial. You need to engage with others to develop your own thinking, understanding and practice. You then synthesise all this learning and experience into your own style of leadership. Do not become a head who feels they have nothing left to learn and whose development is complete. Its not!

So, listen to colleagues, attend meetings, visit other schools, visit other countries, read, get on-line with Twitter and educational blogs, attend conferences, listen and actively engage and contribute. All of this engagement will help shape your thinking, leadership style and philosophies.

Obviously, I have always found writing a great way to formulate and develop my thinking. It's not for everyone, but is another strategy that has worked well for me.

Share!

Developing your school and your leadership is not just about taking and accepting from others. It's a two way process. So you need to be prepared to share.

This means sharing thoughts, thinking, practices, activities and developments. This is something we have not been particularly brilliant at and we need to embrace more willingly. It is so much easier and productive when we are trying to engage with and manage change that we do this in co-operation with others.

If you have developed systems and practices that have been proven to work, you should be prepared to share these with colleagues and within the profession. Better still if you have developed these collaboratively.

How you share is down to you. This might be with neighbouring schools or amongst colleague headteachers you work with or are friends with. More likely it will take place within a group of schools, a Cluster or Learning Community. These are often cross-sector and help to develop understanding and improve transitions for pupils. You may share at a local authority level in a headteacher group or as a member of various working parties that you have an interest in. You could also share at a national level in the same way. You can share by working with other organisations, such as universities, colleges, professional bodies, unions, and so on. You will achieve huge two-way benefits from such sharing, improving your own school or organisation, whilst at the same time contributing to changes in the system and our understanding.

Slow Down!

Anyone involved in education knows that we are constantly dealing with and managing change. Because this is a constant, there is a temptation to try and do too much, too quickly. In that scenario we run the risk of ending up having too much coverage and not enough depth to what we are doing. This will mean there is unlikely to be any lasting benefit for the pupils in your school.

If something is worth changing, then it is worth doing it well and in such a meaningful way that it becomes embedded in practice and the culture of your school or establishment. This means you have to slow down at times and take your time.

Research has demonstrated that any change within a school and classroom can have a positive effect. Trouble is, this effect can rapidly diminish over time, and for lasting impacts to be felt significant change needs to become embedded. The latest concerns over the use of Formative Assessment techniques have demonstrated this.

Dylan William and others have noted that the benefits of Formative Assessment have not been fully achieved in English schools, and others. This is because Formative Assessment was taken on board by government and local authorities, and then advisors distilled it down into a number of strategies and techniques. These were then imparted to teachers and schools via various in-service courses and documents. School Inspectors and others then looked for evidence of these in schools and classrooms.

But in taking this approach, lots of teachers and schools, and those looking at them, lost sight of what was important. William points out that Formative Assessment was supposed to focus on improving learning and teaching experiences and practices. It was also about getting pupils actively engaged with, and understanding of, the learning process. This seems to have been forgotten and so the impact has not been as expected. I am concerned that there is a danger the same thing might happen in Scotland with Curriculum for Excellence and we need to be very wary of this.

The lesson from all of this is that we need to slow down to really achieve meaningful and long-lasting change, and for practitioners to really understand the changes made.

The speed of meaningful change is dictated by the capacity of schools and staff to understand and embed such changes.

That Balance Thing!

I spoke about this earlier, but it needs repeating. I really didn't get balance in my own life right until I was ill for a period of time and had the opportunity to reassess what was going on. Conclusion? My life was out of kilter and lacked equilibrium. Something needed to change.

I had been throwing myself into my role as a teaching headteacher, which meant I had a school to lead, and I was teaching a class three days a week. I was trying to fulfil both roles as well as being very busy outside of school with three growing children, all of who were active in sport and required taxiing to coaching and events all over Scotland, and beyond at times. Basically I was trying to do too much and I needed to take stock and prioritise.

Obviously, my family had to come first. Sometimes we can lose sight of this. Then I had to look at what was going on at work. I realised I couldn't be there for everybody. Indeed, I saw that I needed to delegate more to others to help not only myself, but also to help them develop their leadership skills and experience.

Key also was to slow down and not try to do so much, both at home and at school. I became better at saying no, or not now, and paring back my own workload and expectations.

Guess what? The world didn't end. The school and staff continued to develop, and we continued to improve experiences for all our pupils. We were innovative and reflective and smarter in how we worked. We had a very good HMIe inspection and we were praised for all the development and the opportunities we were offering our learners. I also now had more time and energy for my family and felt better in myself. A true win, win situation.

I insisted all staff also reviewed their own commitments to family and work, and made sure they bought into the philosophy of working hard when at work, but then leaving it when we went home. This is the philosophy I still pursue. We are committed to our professional responsibilities and we work hard as individuals and as a team to achieve our goals. But, when we go home, we concentrate on family, relationships and personal goals. As a result, we continue to develop, move forward and innovate, and staff are happier, less stressed and more balanced in their lives, as am I. Adopting this approach means you and your staff are less likely to experience burnout, and you are more likely to have a positive, focused culture in the workplace.

Order! Order!

Closely linked to getting the work-life balance right, is your ability to prioritise. You have to see the wood from the trees. Prioritising is a key skill that will allow you to achieve what you want to achieve and not be deflected by extraneous matters that might be shoved, or directed, your way.

You ability to prioritise, and give order to tasks, is facilitated by how clear your values, vision and principles are. It is also helped by the effectiveness of your self-evaluation and school development planning. Get all of this right and it is easier to identify what is important.

Get this wrong and everything can feel chaotic, with you being very reactive instead of proactive.
I draw up weekly, and then daily lists of priorities, then work my way through these. If you have done this well, you will know that each task completed is taking you closer to your development and establishment goals.

That is not to say there won't be days when you don't get many, if any, of the tasks on your priority lists completed. That is the nature of school and organisational leadership. In school our priorities will always be the children, parents and staff. The first two can be quite unpredictable and when situations occur which need your immediate attention, you just have to give it. On any one day you can come into work with a list of tasks to be done, but you still have to recognise that these have to be put on hold should more immediate matters call for your attention.

However, you need to get back on track with your priorities as soon as possible.

Everything Changes!

In schools, we constantly have to manage a demanding change agenda. The constant pressure for change can lead to headteachers and schools feeling overwhelmed by all there is to do.

The way to diminish such feelings is twofold.

First, you need to develop a plan to manage the changes. Do not do this in isolation, but in collaboration with your staff and colleagues. A well-crafted implementation plan keeps you in control of events and changes, rather than the other way round.

Secondly, your plan and the implementation will be greatly facilitated if you, and your staff, can see the links between all the changes you need to make, and can also link these to what you are doing already. Failure to make links and connections can lead to changes being seen as more 'things' to do, or 'add-ons' to an already crowded schedule. This in turn leads to superficiality and minimal impact.

For change to be meaningful, implementation has to be planned flexibly and the connections understood by all. When this happens you and your staff are less likely to feel overwhelmed and more likely to feel in control.

All changes should aim to improve outcomes and experiences for pupils. If they are unlikely to do this, you need to consider if they are really necessary and whether you should be expending valuable energy and resources on them?

Pick Your Fights!

Don't waste your energies tackling issues that aren't worth the fight or that you have no chance of winning. Again, if you know your values, vision and principles clearly, this is easier to achieve.

We can all have very firm opinions and views, especially headteachers! What you soon realise is that there are lots of other people who are equally firm and passionate about their own views and opinions. What you have to learn to recognise is when you need to ignore these, confront them, or circumnavigate them in order to still achieve what you and your staff believe to be important.

For instance I have always found it is easy to ignore some personal deficiencies in some teachers if they are excellent practitioners. I have worked with people who are absolutely brilliant teachers, who get the most out of all their children, who are reflective and innovative. Yet these same people can be untidy, lack understanding of other colleagues who they perceive to be not as effective as themselves, can be late for staff meetings or display other personal traits that you might find really annoying in someone who was less effective.

However, if a teacher displays a lack of empathy with pupils, is discriminatory, doesn't follow school policies or practice and is failing their pupils, you are not going to ignore this. You have to deal with it. These kinds of issues you can't ignore and have to tackle or lose your personal and professional credibility.

Similarly, you might come across issues presented by parents or your local authority that you have to face up to if they clash with your personal values, vision or principles. What you quickly realise is that you are never going to win all of these, so what you have to decide is which really matter, and which you are better to compromise on? However, never accept the unacceptable!

Smile!

If you really love your job this bit should be easy. Remember to smile and to take time to thank people for all the hard, and great, work they are doing. We do this all the time with children. It is just as important to do it with all staff.

In my experience, all adults like to be told they are doing a good job. They appreciate that their efforts are recognised and you have noticed. This applies at whatever level they are working at. So make sure you remember this and create time each day to speak to as many of your staff, if not all, and thank them for all that they are doing.

Smile as you move around the school and it becomes infectious. This is a little thing that can lift the atmosphere and mood in the whole organisation

Having a bad day? Take time to sit up straight, take deep breathes and smile. It really does work and will lift your mood and your spirits too.

"Not everything that can be counted counts and not everything that counts can be counted."
Albert Einstein

It Worked For Me!

Main points/principles

- **Deal with issues early when they are small and before they grow**
- **Get out of your office and into corridors and classrooms**
- **Listen to the 'mood music' of your organisation and be prepared to act**
- **Admit what you don't know and be prepared to seek help**
- **If you are developing and innovating, you will make mistakes. Learn from them and don't try to hide them**
- **Look for good ideas and practice and see how they might help you or your school develop**

- Share your practice, ideas and thoughts with others
- Slow down to really embed meaningful change
- Plan flexibly for change to happen and identify connections.
- Remember to get the work/life balance under control
- Prioritise, but people are always the priority
- Pick your fights so as to not waste energy
- Smile!

Conclusion

"To succeed one must be creative and persistent" John H Johnson

Now it is over to you. I hope that what you have read in this book has given you some thoughts to consider, and helps you find a path that is right for you and your leadership development.

Leadership, and particularly school leadership, is not easy. It is complicated and, like learning itself, can be messy. It is challenging of all your faculties, dispositions, and pre-conceptions, as well as your ego. It is demanding and can be quite stressful at times.

So why would anyone undertake it? Well, when you get it right, and sometimes even when you get it wrong, it can be the most fulfilling and satisfying of roles. You are helping to shape the educational experiences and development of all the pupils in your school. You are developing and leading some wonderfully dedicated, inspiring and creative staff in order that they may reach their own potential. You are contributing to the development and understanding in education, as a whole and, perhaps most importantly, you are making a difference.

Don't be put off by the doubters, cynics and those who question you and your desire to lead. School leadership is not for everyone but hopefully you are, or will become, one of those that find themselves and their passion within the role.
I know I have.

"Keep away from those who try to belittle your ambitions. Small people always do that, but the really great make you believe that

you too can become great." Mark Twain

Bibliography and Suggested Reading

I have read lots of books on Education and leadership. Equally, I have heard lots of people speak on these issues. Below is a list of some of the ones that have had the biggest impact on me, personally and professionally. You could do a lot worse than read some of these to help develop your own thinking and find your own paths.

Paul Black and Dylan William *Inside The Black Box*

Chris Barez-Brown *Shine-How To Survive and Thrive At Work*

234

Brian Boyd *The Learning Classroom*

Graham Donaldson for the Scottish Government *Teaching Scotland's Future*

Michael Fullan *What's Worth Fighting For in Headship?*

Reuven Feuerstein Y Rand and Ra S Feuerstein *The Feuerstein Instrumental Enrichment Program*

Howard Gardner *Frames Of Mind-The Theory Of Multiple Intelligences*

Malcolm Gladwell *Outliers-The Story of Success*

John Hattie *Visible Learning for Teachers*

George Kohlrieser *Hostage at The Table*

Barbara MacGilchrist Jane Reed and Kate Myres *The Intelligent School*

Barbara MacGilchrist and Margaret Buttress *Transforming Learning and Teaching*

Geoff Petty *Teaching Today*

Ken Robinson *Out of Our Mind-Learning to be Creative* and *The Element-How Finding You Passions Changes Everything*

Scottish Government *Curriculum for Excellence-Building The Curriculum Documents 1-5*

Alistair Smith Mark Lovatt and Derek Wise *Accelerated Learning-A Users Guide*

Alistair Smith Mark Lovatt and John Turner *Learning To Learn-The L2 Approach*

Rupert Wegerif *Mind Expanding-Teaching For Thinking and Creativity In Primary Education*

George Gilchrist November 2012